D0105071

letters to a young golfer

Bob Duval

with Carl Vigeland

letters to a young golfer

afterword by David Duval

A Member of the Perseus Books Group

Published by Basic Books,
A Member of the Perseus Books Group

Designed by Rick Pracher

Cataloging-in-Publication Data is available at the Library of Congress.
ISBN 0-465-01738-X

02 03 04 05 / 10 9 8 7 6 5 4 3 2 1

for Tripp

Life is way too hard and way too short,
not to play golf.

—Arnold Palmer

Contents

Acknowledgments

Both Bob and Carl want to say a special thank you to young golfers John Donatich and Lucienne Wu at Basic Books, Jack McKeown, and also Jamie Brickhouse, Angela Baggetta, and John Hughes; to Wayne Kabak at the William Morris Agency; Lori Hobkirk and Jane Raese at The Book Factory; and Nick Samuels; to Tammy Blake; and to James Dodson, author of *The Dewsweepers*, for his kind permission to use the Arnold Palmer quotation at the beginning of this book. Carl also thanks his son Christian, Bonnie and Alistair Catto, Julie Cowan, Dave Barbosa, Happi Cramer, Rob Gibson, Jonathan Klate, Mark Klingensmith, Mary Lapinski, Vikki Lenhart, Tracy Mehr, Phelicia, John L. Prinzivalli, Andrea Schulz, Sheldon, Al Sorenson, Kim Townsend, David Twohig, and WM. Bob would like to thank all the people in this book, including Brett and Jamie Simon, two members of his family whose presence was felt but not mentioned, and most of all his wife, best friend and partner, on the golf course and off, Shari Duval.

Introduction
We are all young golfers

New Year's Day, 2002

Dear Reader,

We are all young golfers. Every time I play golf I think to myself, "I'm starting from scratch again. This is another opportunity to play good." If a golf score were cumulative, so the score from each round was added to the next, I don't know who would ever have the courage to play.

You learn to hit a golf ball through mechanics, but that isn't how you play golf. Swinging a club and playing golf are not the same thing. Naturally the two are related, but there are plenty of people with good swings—even at the professional level—who don't really know how to play golf. They look great on the range, but as soon as the match begins something happens to them, they make bad decisions or doubt themselves at a crucial moments, they lose the very thing that got them there. On the other hand, to judge by their performance in tournament play, some of the greatest golfers in the world don't possess what you might term a perfect swing. Lee Trevino takes the club way outside on his backswing; Arnold Palmer has that funny move with his forearms on his follow-through. But look at their records. If I hit a bad shot—and I hit plenty of them, everyone does—I immediately start putting it behind me, because you never know what may happen *next*—in golf, or in life. This is a book about dealing with the mistakes we make and the surprises we find in golf—how we handle the unknown in the game and, more fundamentally, the mysterious, unpredictable, thrilling discoveries about ourselves we can all make if we work hard and learn to enjoy what we're doing. My anticipation of the unexpected, my experience with the pains as well as the joys of life—these inform everything I do on the golf course. I am a man first, a golfer second.

Long before I hit my first shot in a golf tournament that mattered, I lost a person I loved more than life itself. His name was Brent Duval and he was my oldest child. He was twelve years old when he died. You never really get over the death of a child. To this day, being reminded of Brent's death makes me feel so vulnerable. It also makes me remember how grateful I am to be here. Each day. Each round. Each shot.

When people ask me about my life, how I figured out finally how to keep going, I'm quick to say I'm not a hero. "Don't put me on a pedestal," I say. We all live with some kind of pain. Learning how to do that, rather than trying to make it go away, took me many years and many tries.

My name is Bob Duval. I am fifty-five years old. My only daughter, Deirdre, has just graduated from college with a second degree in psychology; my surviving son David and I play golf for a living. David is thirty as I write this—thirty and just coming into his own as one of the best golfers of his generation. I used to say I taught David everything he knows, but that's not true anymore, if it ever was. David still calls when something goes out of sync, and we play when we're home in Ponte Vedra, Florida (his house is about a mile from mine). But what he has achieved in the last few years—winning nearly a dozen tournaments in a sequence of fewer than three dozen starts (including one in which he shot a record-breaking, final-round score of 59), and dramatically capturing the 2001 British Open, his first major—I cannot explain these achievements by discussing his grip or stance, his ball alignment, his swing.

David was always competitive as a boy, at one time playing as much baseball as golf, but "competitive" doesn't begin to explain the mastery—in one such stretch, the domination—which he plays with now. I wish I could cite a specific something I once said or recall a specific something I showed him, but learning to play golf, at whatever level you play, doesn't work like that.

You hang together, father and son, you play all those

evenings in the spring after school, you see him at the club every day during the summer, you hit balls together, hundreds of balls a day, you watch him grow, you help him get into tournaments and, later, college; you try to be there for him. And when in those hard nights he remembers, in the days and months and finally years, you try to say what cannot be said. You comfort, you encourage, you endure. You tell him to go on.

"Play what's in front of you, David."

And then it hits you, a realization comes over your whole body so you feel it even in your swing, sending range balls into the distance on a summer afternoon at a country club in New Jersey, where the Senior Tour is competing one week, or at home at the TPC Stadium course, where David and I are practicing. The feeling starts somewhere in your gut and travels throughout your body, to your arms and legs, making them weightless. Suddenly I am light-headed. I stand still. More than 200 yards away I see a clearing by some trees. I've been hitting three-woods toward that clearing. I take a deep breath, then another. I can feel the tension in me, the trigger that I'm going to be playing, begin to disappear. By the time I hit the first shot off the first tee it will be gone, except for the adrenaline flow when your name is going up the leader board.

At Desert Mountain in Arizona, the first time I played in a major championship on the Senior Tour, I cold-topped my first drive. We were using split tees that day—half the field starting on the front nine, half on the back—and my group was beginning on the 10th tee. We were downwind, so I took a three-wood to keep it in the fairway. Well, that was the intention. Much to my chagrin, I topped the ball into a cactus plant—a distance of about thirty or forty steps!—where it was unplayable. So I had to retreive it and, with all my options exhausted, return to the tee and add a stroke. As I walked back through the cactus to hit another drive, while the next group was already waiting to tee off, the starter raised his voice to the surprised gallery: "Now at the tee—for the second time—Bob Duval."

It helps to have a sense of humor, because golf is a solitary game. No one can make the swing for you, whether you're trying to qualify for the pro tour or beat your buddy for a beer. But we golfers are part of a community, the huge group of diverse people who love and play this often maddening, ultimately exhilarating game.

In my own career, and in my life, other people have been there when I've needed them. But you must take that first step. Before you can ask someone else for help, you must know what you're looking for.

For me, after a lifetime of teaching golf, this meant I had to ask myself a terrifying yet liberating question: Could I do something in middle age that I'd feared doing as a young man after college? It was David who put that question to me, as his career on the PGA Tour was just beginning to take off.

When I was teaching him to play golf, I used to tell him, "Your score is just a succession of numbers. Don't add them up until your round is done." I still say the same thing to David and myself—and to you: Don't dwell on what just happened, whether it was great or terrible. Move on. Play the next shot.

That's advice I had to follow myself when I qualified for the Senior Tour, or I'd still be giving golf lessons for a living. Or maybe I'd have become a fishing guide, something I considered when I hurt my elbow two years ago (and then, after it healed following surgery, I injured a shoulder). The fact that I'm playing for lots of money today isn't the result of some magic spell or simple good fortune. I didn't win the lottery (though sometimes, with the prizes they pay out here, it might seem like I did). I was already lucky to have lived my entire life teaching and playing a game I love. But when I left behind the steady paycheck of my last teaching position, I knew that the only way I was going to make it was to develop a method, a habit of being prepared, that would carry me forward and through the most nerve-racking golf adventure of my life. I had to put a target in my mind, like the target you aim for and react to on each golf shot, and then stay focused on it through the ups and downs that I knew I would face.

Just about every week on the Senior Tour someone playing in a pro-am will ask me for advice about becoming professional.

"How long have you been playing golf?" I ask.

Typically, the answer is vague, and when I see the person take a few swings it's pretty obvious what kind of a game he or she has. But every so often someone who can really hit the ball might have what it takes to become a pro.

"Have you played in some tournaments?" I ask.

"Yeah, club champion at home, and a couple of years ago I qualified for my state amateur. I'm also hoping to get into this year's U.S. Public Links."

"Well," I think to myself, "what do I say now?" Because there's no way of sugarcoating a reality: Playing golf at the highest level is ultimately a head game. And you don't learn that by perfecting a beautiful swing on a range, or by beating all your friends in a Nassau, or even by competing in some fairly rigorous amateur competitions where you live. You do it, as you do anything substantive in life, by repeatedly and incrementally growing through a long, arduous process of big failures and small successes, until one day the pieces fall together—the short game and the long irons, course management and competitive strategy—and suddenly you realize, "I can play golf."

Of course, most golfers aren't trying to become professionals. But everybody wants to improve. Having fun with something usually means getting better at it, whether you're a pro or a beginner. That means you, Susan in seventh grade in Boise, Joe at his club in Boston, Dr. Meredith leaving work in Dallas. But don't fear some failure along the way.

Like that story in the Bible says, you have to lose yourself to find yourself. In golf we call that experience my cold-topped drive at that first major, all those tournaments I lost before I finally won. Anyone who has ever played this game has felt the uncertainty, the nervousness, even the reservations that can creep up on you out of nowhere. Maybe the biggest difference between people who play golf for a living and people who play golf for fun is that a professional gets these feelings before he or she plays, while other golfers get them *while* they're playing. To learn the difference and how to overcome it, you have to develop a routine, you have to practice that routine, so that it becomes second nature. Once I was playing with another pro who put his club back in the bag and started his routine from scratch after someone walked across the fairway before his swing.

When you've done your routine, you've made all the decisions about the shot you're going to hit—and all that is left for you to do is visualize. Pick the club and go. If you don't pull off the shot you planned, put its memory in the back of your mind until after the round, because the last thing any golfer wants to be *thinking* about when he or she is playing golf is . . . golf.

I'd better repeat that: You do your analyzing, your checking when you are practicing, not when you are playing. On the course during a round, you think about the shot you want to play, where you want the ball to go—and that is all. It would be like someone playing a musical instrument or flying a plane. You play scales when you are practicing, but during a performance you concentrate on the music, you sing the song. And when you bring in that 747 you keep your eye on the runway, not on the flight manual.

Very few things in golf, or life, work out perfectly, and I'd feel really good if the person reading these letters discovered how the professional goes through the same travails and doubts as everyone else but then bounces back. I think inevitably you must fail before you succeed, not just because there is no such thing as perfection in golf but because success—or, more accurately, fulfillment—rests so much on your response to the myriad of problems built into the basics of the game. It's easy to get lost in the vast and conflicting schools of thought regarding technique and mechanics. But that all goes out the window anyway once you're playing. Then it's just you. You and that bad lie. You and the putt you just missed. You and the pond guarding the green, the one where your ball made such a splendid splash. What are you going to do about it, now? Are you going to feel sorry for yourself, or try again? Are you going to give up or continue?

Resilience. That's what the letters in this book are really about—how we can help one another to grow, to achieve our true potential, and take pleasure in the game and the company it gives us the opportunity to keep.

Play on,

Bob

■ **A note to the readers of these letters:** If there's one thing golfers like even more than playing golf, it's talking about golf. The people I'm talking with here in these letters include several members of my family—my second wife Shari, my son David, my daughter Deirdre, my older brother Jim (aka Elf, also a golf teaching professional in Florida) and his oldest son Scott, a business executive with Coca-Cola in Atlanta—and a number of my friends: Colin Armstrong, who lives at Plantation Country Club, the last golf course where I was the teaching pro; John Donatich, who inspired me to become a young writer; near neighbor Michele Goff, who runs a thriving corporate workshop business that sometimes takes her husband Murray away from his piano; Hubert Green, my Florida State classmate and two-time major tournament winner; Jeremy MacDonald, who was my last assistant at Plantation before I left; and Robert Moore, M.D., who still lives in the Old Ortega neighborhood where my children grew up, and plays golf at Timuquana Country Club where I held my first head pro position.

letters to a young golfer

Bob Duval with David, age 8, in 1980.

You hang together, father and son, you play all those evenings in the spring after school, you see him at the club every day during the summer, you hit balls together, hundreds of balls a day, you watch him grow, you help him get into tournaments and, later, college; you try to be there for him.

Part ONE

Letters to My Son David

1 I was so proud of you

July 23, 2001

Dear David,

Too bad they didn't televise the award ceremonies after you made that last putt. I would have been curious to know what you said when they presented you with the claret jug. I would have been speechless. I know I was that Sunday when we had our father-son doubleheader two years ago, when I won the Emerald Coast the same day you did the Players Championship. Do you remember what you told me the night before? "Go out and play, Dad," you said. "You're going to think about what a win will mean for you. Okay. Do it. But then think about your next shot. Just take one shot at a time." Well, you followed your own advice at the British Open. I was so proud of you!

I was home instead of playing because the shoulder is really bothering me now. Had some more tests and will probably go in for the surgery next month, after we play together in the Fred Meyer Challenge. Looking forward to that; don't think I've played before in Oregon. Hopefully I can help our team; have had to manufacture a backswing where I don't take the club much above my shoulders, so it's not too painful. Might still blow it by you.

When the coverage ended before your speech I turned off the TV and we took Buddy outside—me and Shari and the dog. Walked to the dock. Took a bottle of Dom Perignon I'd been saving. Standing on the dock, I was thinking about all the great shots you made at Royal Lytham. That putt for birdie at the 13th, after you'd bogeyed the 12th, looked about 11, 12 feet; that was some putt. When I was watching it on television, Colin called me on his cell phone. He didn't go to the course that day, stayed at a friend's house and watched it on BBC.

"Laddy," he said to me. "I think Sonny's going to do it."

"Yeah, Colin. But he's just hit into the deep rough on fifteen. Looks like he's got at least 200 yards to the green." I didn't know that the American television feed was on a slight tape delay; Colin was watching live.

"He's already hit the next shot, Bobby. Stiff!"

And then I saw it, too. Damn. Made me think of those times when you were a kid coming over to Timuquana. Remember how we'd go out in the evening, after I'd finished teaching? We'd hit all those goofy shots—big slices, big hooks, hitting through branches, running the ball through a bunker, skipping it over the lake.

That was after Brent died. Thought about him today, too. Thought about all those years ago, and now I'm standing on the end of our dock, next to that boat you gave me, just me and Shari drinking that champagne. And Buddy, except Buddy doesn't drink. Taught him a lot of tricks; haven't been able to teach him that one.

Anyway, you're on a different plane now. You know you can do it, because you have done it. What perfect timing, just before turning thirty. I'm going to save some of this champagne for when you get back; you'd better bring that claret jug, that trophy, with your name on it and all those other names—Hagen, Hogan, Jack, the King, Watson, Gary, Tiger—you bring that jug and I'll bring the champagne.

Love,
Dad

2
The weather in my mind is Scotland's

July 24

Dear David,

I know you're on your way home so I'll probably see you at the party before you read this. It's pretty early, a warm, muggy morning, but the weather in my mind is Scotland's, misty and cool and the cold water of the Irish Sea lapping along the shore near the ruins of Robert the Bruce's castle, next to the ninth fairway of Turnberry's Ailsa course. That's the one where I tried to qualify for the '77 British Open, during the period in my teaching life when I also was playing some of my best golf. I didn't make it, but my old Florida State college classmate Hubert Green was already in. And then he finished third, although he was far back of Nicklaus and Watson. I stayed over, already had my ticket, and I followed along in the gallery when Hubert had it going.

The castle—Robert the Bruce's—is next to a lighthouse. Right on the edge of the land, you could see an opening in the foundation where boats must have come in hundreds of years ago. Only one wall, part of it, still standing. Ailsa Craig, this huge granite boulder of an island, in the mist out in the sea, toward Ireland. The wind was something.

So, now, it's you.

Love,
Dad

3
Dad was a hard worker

August 1

Dear David,

Up here outside New York for something called the Lightpath Long Island Classic. It's the one Dana Quigley won four years ago—his first victory on the Senior Tour—and as he came off the 18th green they told him his father had just died. You know Dana's nephew, Brett, who plays on the Buy.com Tour and some regular Tour events. Dana played, too, a generation ago, didn't make much money—what happens to most guys who try professional golf—and went home to New England, where he became a club pro and competed in regional events. Then he came out on the Senior Tour and found a whole new game and life.

Shot a 75 today, very disappointing. Wish it was like one of those times when you ask me to watch you and I say, "Your hands are too low," and as soon as you correct that, bingo!, everything's right. It's the putting that's been letting me down, and I know why. With the kind of game I'm playing until this shoulder gets fixed, it's hard to hit it consistently close. I'm hitting fewer greens in regulation—statistically, I'm down about three percentage points, and you know what that means. Those three points are the difference between winning and showing up, because with all the subsequent pressure on my putting, I'm not scoring as well as I did before I got hurt.

I don't care who you are or what you do, in the long run there has to be balance—in your game and your life. You can't rely on one thing in golf, like making one-putts because you're missing greens and therefore chipping when you should be putting. That's why I'm glad I kept playing all those years I was teaching as a club pro; never could be doing what I'm doing now if it hadn't been for that. It's too hard to compete at this level. Whatever level golfer you are, you have to play.

I suppose that was what got your grandfather Hap to keep that job at the post office all those years when he was the pro at Stanford. Been thinking about him this week, we're only a few hours from Schenectady. Home. Well, original home.

Back there in Schenectady, in the winter, there was no golf, of course. So things were a little easier to manage during those months. But then, once spring came, Hap would get up at 4:30 in the morning so that he could be at the post office a full day and then get off at two in the afternoon and go to the golf course. He'd always have lessons to give, somedays all afternoon until dark. Your grandmother worked in the golf shop in the daytime, but Hap had an assistant pro, Dick Osborne, to help with some of the golf stuff—tournaments, clinics, that sort of thing. I saw Dickie a couple of years ago at an outing and we talked about Hap. Man, Hap worked hard.

He'd get two bucks a lesson, maybe. Can you imagine that? I used to shag balls for him. Your Uncle Jim and I would alternate days and that's how we earned our spending money. We didn't have those tractors to pickup the balls. Jim and I ran along with the shag bag, watching so we wouldn't get hit out there in the field between the 18th and 8th where Hap always gave his lessons. In the summer it seemed like we just picked up balls all day. Hap would count the balls we shagged, and if one was missing he deducted a nickel from the twenty-five cents a lesson we got for shagging (every now and then we'd get fifty cents from a big spender). The person taking the lesson would pay my dad and dad paid us, but sometimes the student would also give a tip. For a day we might make four or five dollars. But if we wanted anything, Hap would sometimes pay for it. One summer Jimmy and I saved up enough to buy a new bicycle that we were going to share, and Hap chipped in to buy a second, so we'd each have new bikes.

I remember we rode those bikes to the golf course from home after school. We lived on the outskirts of the city in an area called Woodlawn. We'd take the back roads and then have to cross State Street. That's Route 9 now, the connector between Albany and Schenectady. When we weren't shagging balls we were allowed to play golf.

Even in the wintertime Hap would give lessons. If the weather was bad, he'd teach indoors. He'd start right after Christmas, working for the department of parks and recreation in the city, the school system, the Jewish Community Center, and the YMCA. It was one of those programs like every community seems to have for learning the guitar, Spanish, ballroom dancing. You know, extension programs. Hap did golf. He'd teach three sessions a night, each an hour long, starting at seven, and eight, and nine. Then he'd stop for a chocolate soda or piece of pie and coffee on his way home and get to bed for a few hours before starting up at the post office the next morning.

This was in the late 1950s, just before I was a teenager. Hap was in the army reserve, too. He had a heart problem all his life, a murmur, so he couldn't be drafted. Instead, he enlisted in the army reserve.

From everything he did he saved his money, I mean really saved it, David. He'd save enough money to buy a new car every two years. Cash. Saved enough to buy a house. He put a good chunk down on it. It wasn't a big house, but it was our house.

What a feeling of pride when I went back years later to visit it. But wistful, too. Our house was still there. I couldn't get over how really small it was. Two bedrooms, a living room, a bathroom, and a kitchen. Jim and I shared a room, and our parents were just down the hallway. That's the way a lot of people lived then. Still do.

During the Depression, when no one else in his family could get work, Hap earned fifteen dollars a week. He gave it to his mother. All his brothers were bricklayers and there was no work for them. Their mother would give Hap all the hand-me-down clothes from the other brothers. Imagine: He'd buy new clothes for the older brothers and then he'd get their hand-me-downs. I'm the younger brother in my family, but sometimes when I think about it, it seems like all I did was goof off, shag balls, and play golf when I could. When you have kids I bet they'll want to spend all their time on the Internet. By the way, do you know how to get on the Internet yet?

Did I ever tell you what it was like to play golf at a high school run by the Christian Brothers of Ireland? One of the brothers, Brother Cotter, was the coach. He was strict and tough, he slapped me around a few times. But he really loved golf. I played some basketball, too, intramural stuff, but I wasn't really tall enough, and, besides, golf was consuming. Sometimes the coach and a few of the other brothers would come over to the house. They liked to drink, too, they were a funny bunch. And there was a golf course right behind the school, so we didn't play at Stanford all the time. That course is still there, too; where the Schenectady Blue Jays used to play, a local businessman had built a golf course around the stadium and the stadium was the club house after the Blue Jays left. So it was called the Stadium Golf Club. There was a par–three practice area where the old baseball infield was. If we ever get back there for something like that charity skins game we played a while ago, I'll have to take you over this time. It's a long way from Royal Lytham and St. Anne's.

That's all gone for me now. And Hap, too, dead for ten years. I felt so bad, how you lost both your grandfathers within three days of each other. You played a lot of golf at Fernandina Beach with Grandad Harry; it's such a pity that Hap lived too far away for the two of you to get a chance to play golf together. When he became sick and moved into our guest house, it was too late. If he could have seen you with that claret jug! All those times we used to watch those tournaments, and Jack won, or Arnie. I know the old Stanford guys watched the British Open. I still hear from a few of them. And still run into people in every part of the country who either took a lesson from Hap or knew him, or their fathers knew him. That's how the line runs. It's like a good putt, straight and true.

See you in Oregon,
Dad

4

That space somewhere inside you

August 10

Dear David,

Well, we played pretty good, didn't we? Twenty-one under par for two rounds but we finished third. That Brad Faxon can putt; he was making stuff from everywhere. It got me to thinking again why, at every level of golf, certain players fail while others succeed. And I still think the best way to explain it is there are no limits in golf, so the question you're always asking yourself is, "How low can I score?" In every other sport, high score wins. It's more than the logic of the game, it's a complete mindset. Simplify. Get rid of the extraneous, the mistakes. Make your shots with less conscious effort. When you're playing in this zone, there is such a flow of positive thoughts that failure is not an option. Everything is in tune.

You know, when even Nicklaus boasts in his book—the autobiography he wrote a few years ago—that only a handful of pro golfers truly understand their swings, it makes me wonder if a full explanation of success in golf lies beyond our knowledge. We put such a premium on perfection, but even the greatest golfers in the world lose more often than they win. I used to remind my students that even though Sam Snead captured a career record eighty-one victories, including eleven in 1950 (the last time any player won at least ten in a single season), he never won the United States Open. And Tom Watson, who won the Senior PGA this year, struggled early in his career until, he says, "I learned how to win and believe in myself." Later, after all those British Opens and regular tour victories, he went something like nine years between victories. Even Jack, whose twenty major tournament titles are still the record, missed the cut sometimes. It makes you ponder what it is that has made the great players great.

Maybe you don't like to think like this in case it's going to spook you. Now that I'm going to be laid up for five months after this operation, I'm going to have lots of opportunities to reflect.

"When I started out on the Tour I believed I had progressed a fair distance along [the] learning curve," Jack wrote. Did you read it? A little dry in places, and long descriptions of golf rounds, but there's some pretty neat stuff there, like when he describes how he learned to make his own corrections, "in effect, to teach myself, to have sufficient mental grasp of the proper technique." Only then did he begin to become Jack. I mean, the Jack we knew when he was in his prime. "In short," he said, "I'd been playing too long with crutches." I think he meant that his longtime teacher and mentor, Jack Grout, couldn't be with him while he was actually playing. To discard those "crutches" without discarding what he had learned from Grout—to trust what he had learned "was to gain the independence that comes from truly understanding the game's cause and effect oneself, alone and unaided." No handholding, so to speak.

Man, that's some phrase: alone and unaided. To me, really, every golfer must find more than his swing; you need to know who you are on the golf course (and probably off). You need to know and believe in your golfing self. But getting there is so elusive!

"I haven't heard anything new about the golf swing since I was a pro," Gary Player says. I know what he means. So many of my students used to think the answer to their problem was going to be found in a manual or a diagram. I get so amused when I hear about someone teaching golf by saying your arms should be at three o'clock, nine o'clock. I was talking about it one day on the range with Orville Moody, whose only victory when he was a regular Tour player was the U.S. Open.

"So, my arms are supposed to be where?" Sarge said. We call him Sarge because he served in the U.S. Army before coming out on tour. "What if I don't have a watch on me?"

The great player overcomes the anguish of his mistakes. That's why I was so thrilled with you playing at Royal Lytham; the year before at St. Andrews, when you lost to Tiger, when you finally needed, what was it, four strokes to get out of that big old bunker next to the road by the 17th green—you took the loss and you came back.

Maybe none of us truly realize we've attained what we've been striving for until we're there. But then you're faced with the fresh challenge of sustaining. Dealing with the demon of success. It's amazing to me, almost paradoxical: Without good form and technique it's virtually impossible to succeed. But form itself doesn't win championships. I probably never told you this, but long before I won that tournament two years ago at Emerald Coast, I used to leave your mother and you and your brother and sister and play someplace for cash—cash on the table, or in someone's pocket. Those were the stakes, whatever someone put up himself. You learned to play then, or you came home to your family broke. That was when I had to make all the parts work together, to deal with the adversity of the game on my own.

As you can imagine, or maybe remember, I didn't always win. Somedays the game won. Still does. And I suppose even the best players often find the game as baffling as everyone else. When that occurs, how do they—we, anyone who plays—find ways to return to the source of our secrets? Let me answer my own question. Success isn't having a great grip or beautiful stance, but something deeper, something more basically related, in the case of grip of stance, to an approach to grip and stance and ball position and all the other things.

One night I was practicing bunker shots at the TPC, something I've done countless times. And my cell phone rang. Talking, I held the phone in my left hand while I kept hitting bunker shots with my right, and the balls started stopping closer to the pin. When that happens, when you cease to worry about results, you're in a place, an invisible space somewhere inside you. To play great golf you build with your physical strengths or talent on that invisible foundation. As you, too, know David, the struggle is always internal, and always alone. It comes like it did for me that night in a TPC practice bunker, or on camera before millions of people watching a tournament, but it doesn't happen "out there." It's *here*, the essence of yourself. I always thought it was neat that in golf we say you go out on the front nine and then come back on the inward nine—home.

Enough philosophizing. I'll be going in for the surgery next week. Thanks so much for offering to send your plane to pick me up and take me back to Jacksonville after the operation. Hap would have gotten a kick out of that—you and your own plane. Of course it makes sense as a business decision. But it must be pretty nice, too.

Wish I knew how this injury happened, maybe I hurt it after recovering from last year's elbow, but nothing to do now except keep going. Never was.

Hey, did I ever tell you what that starter said to me and my buddies, in Ireland, the year you played in the Walker Cup, and we stopped to play a round at Royal County Down? One of the guys hit a poor first drive, so like most Americans, he reached into his pocket for another ball. And the starter, who was also the club secretary, was having none of it.

"Fore, please," he shouted. "Ball's in play."

The guy didn't have any idea what was going on.

"Hey, dummy," one of us said. "The starter means there are no Mulligans in Ireland."

Love,
Dad

Bob Duval in action today.

Pick the club and go. If you don't pull off the shot that you planned, put its memory in the back of your mind until after the round, because the last thing any golfer wants to be thinking about when he or she is playing golf is . . . golf.

Part TWO

LETTERS TO MY FRIENDS AND FAMILY

5
Moving on

January 2, 2001

Dear Colin,

We made it to another one. For me these commemorations have never been quite what everyone seems to make of them. You know me; I'm not a big one for looking back. It's poison in your golf game, and I'm not sure what purpose it serves in your life. As soon as I look back I start missing everyone. And if you spend too much time thinking about what might have been in golf you'll drive yourself crazy. Looking back means you take yourself too seriously, you're making too much of something that happened, like anyone could care about that putt you missed. No one else cares after the shot is over; you shouldn't care, either. "Come on, laddy, get on with it!" I can hear you saying to me. It's like you have to take things seriously and not seriously at the same time. Do you see the connection?

Still—can I contradict myself?—I woke up this morning, let Buddy out, and for some reason started thinking about how long we've known each other, how many years it's been since you took your first lesson from me at Timuquana. (And now you win my money; I may be giving you too many strokes.) We never say this sort of thing when we're over at Pablo or playing at the TPC, but I'm still so amazed at what you've achieved—on the golf course and off. How you built that computer business so successfully, just like you built your golf game, step by step. And then said, "Ok, that's it. Now I'm going to do what I want to." And you have—you've made your life into one grand celebration of your friendships. All the friends you bring over from England every year to play golf, the house you rent for everyone . . . and you won't take a penny from one of them, except on the golf course. How you are always there for your friends. How you were there for me when I was at my low point after my first marriage ended, wondering where I was going, giving golf lessons every day. And you were one of the people who said to me when I started to think about quitting my job and trying to make it as a Senior Tour player, "Do it. Give it a try, Bobby," and now here I am, five years on the Senior Tour and counting (though last season didn't seem like much of a year with all the problems I was having with that elbow; glad I got it fixed, feels brand new in fact, can't wait to get out there again).

It's always seemed to me the greatest thing about golf, such a solitary game, with everyone on his own, yet the people you play with, compete against, become your friends. It's even like that on the Senior Tour; not with everyone, of course, there are jerks there like anywhere else. But really, when you stop to think about it, what an amazing game. You try your damndest to beat the heck out of someone and then afterward you buy him a drink. I might even buy you one the next time we play.

Buddy didn't want to come in so I took my coffee out to the dock. Can't believe we're in the new house; still so much to do, and the place on Neptune Beach still to sell, but we're in. Like house, like golf. Just as something always needs fixing around home, in golf if the short game's good, you probably need to work on your long irons, if you're driving the ball great, like I was the other day at the TPC Stadium Course, then it's like, "When am I going to make a putt?"

Speaking of the TPC, it's funny how everyone talks about the back nine, especially the finishing holes with the island green on seventeen and that cool drive if you take a shorter route on eighteen. That means driving along or even over the water, if you're going to cut it back into the fairway, or out toward the bank if you're going to draw it back in. That's where the crowd sits during the tournament. And if you aim right, you'd better be sure it starts right, because anything dead center can hook into the water if you're not careful. Those holes are great but I've always liked the front nine almost as much: the tee shot on the short, 380-yard fourth. I like how you come out of the chute with trees and water in front of the tee and guarding the right side of the fairway. You can't be long or left because then you've got a sidehill lie for your second shot.

It's the strategy of the hole that I love. I remember what Jack Nicklaus taught David in the 1992 U.S. Open at Pebble Beach. David had already met Jack—one of Jack's sons went to Georgia Tech—and Jack had invited David to play a practice round with him at Pebble after David qualified for the tournament. I was along for the ride as my son's caddy. Anyway, we got to the famous 18th, with the sweeping dogleg left of that narrow fairway along the Pacific, and Jack asked David how he thought you should play the hole. Just the way Jack said it, you could tell it was something he'd already given much thought to, going back to the many tournaments he'd played there, including the famous U.S. Open in 1982, when Tom Watson chipped in on the 17th to beat Jack for the title.

"There's a sprinkler head out there at one hundred and two yards to the center of the green," Jack said to David. "Your goal on the tee here is to get to that sprinkler head in two shots." Just about no one back then reached Pebble's 18th green in two; you had to play three shots to the green.

"So," Jack continued, "you can hit a three-wood and a six-iron, or maybe two four-irons . . . there's lots of combinations. You want to choose the one you're most comfortable with, that you're most certain of executing correctly, and then play accordingly." That was a real lesson for David from maybe the greatest thinker the game has ever had.

Remembering that day, and thinking about the fourth at the TPC Stadium Course makes me want to tee one up right now. I'm not sure how I'd handle Pebble, but at the TPC fourth I always hit three-wood or driver, depending on the wind, cut it a little, and then an eight- or nine-iron or wedge over the water guarding the green to the pin. Sweet.

When the Players Championship moved over to the TPC from Sawgrass in the early 1980s—just after Brent died and I was still at Timuquana—we'd come down to watch, usually on a practice day. Later, after I moved to Plantation and David was beginning to play more, he used to work the tournament as a standard bearer, you know, carrying the scoreboard for a twosome. And now, not many years later, he's a winner of the tournament.

It's nice being so near the TPC in our new house. When we're home, I can go over there and practice anytime I want. The other day I was working on nothing but long bunker shots. Lot of guys when they're teaching focus on the ball position, putting the ball back in your stance a bit and then you want to make contact with the ball first, not with the sand. When it's a long shot like that it's all true, but I never saw anyone pull off a long bunker shot when it mattered just because they did that. In fact, if you start thinking about all those things when you're playing you might even miss the ball. You think about them when you're practicing—a lot. But once you're playing, you need to keep the same attitude, the same confidence, the same feeling whether you've got a great lie in the middle of the fairway or a greenside bunker shot, like the one I had that day on the par-five ninth at the TPC after I was feeling silly and tried to hit that narrow little green in two.

I miss being so close to the ocean—now we're a mile away instead of a hundred yards—but you know me, I've never stayed in one place too long. Just like my golf game, I guess.

This reflecting is making me thirsty. What do they call those things with the olives in them?

Bobby

6

The greatest prize

January 3

Dear Deirdre,

Meant to write yesterday; it was so great to have you around for a few days, you seem on top of the world with everything at school. Hearing you talk about it made me remember more than thirty years ago when Uncle Jim was thinking of going to Florida State but then he got a partial scholarship for golf. I never gave it a thought at the time, but things were already moving on for me then. I've never said much about this part of my life to you—you weren't even on the scene yet—and then later it seems like I was always too busy to sit down and just tell you about it. There are still things in my dad's life I wish I knew, like the period before he settled down in Schenectady and lived out west. He even tried the pro tour then, but I never remember his talking about it. So, here goes, a little family history.

Uncle Jim—Jimmy to me—never liked to compete as much as I did when we were growing up. But he played golf well enough that Hugh Durham, the Florida State golf coach, contacted me about going to college with Jimmy and playing golf there, too. You couldn't compete in those days in the U.S. juniors unless you were a member of a private country club, but Coach Durham had seen me play in the International Jaycees tournament. I'd got beaten at the finals of the New York State junior by Carl De Caesar, and Carl also ended up going to Florida State on a golf scholarship. He was from Rochester, a few hours west of Schenectady. Another New York guy, Dave Philo, was already down there; Dave's Uncle Jim's age. So then in came Carl De Caesar, Jay Morelli, Jim Conace, Denny Lyons from Jamestown, and me—it was like a whole New York team. Dave Philo's brother Ron and Uncle Jim were on the team, too.

And then Hubert Green arrived. He broke our New York string; he was from Birmingham, Alabama. We gave him so much grief about that, which was funny because we were all Yankees and here we are at a southern school. Once we wouldn't give him a ride when we passed him hitchhiking. He could get angry, but it didn't bother his golf. But you could tell right away that Hubert had a game.

Freshman year we rotated—I would play first, Carl second, Hubert played third, then we'd change the order. Hubert went home that summer and played the amateur circuit in his area. He won the Southern Amateur Championship, and when he came back to school, nobody could beat him anymore. That's how good he was. He went on to be an All-American. He had such fast hands when he came through the ball. He generated astonishing clubhead speed with the release of those hands. Still does.

I had spent that summer after freshman year like I would all my college summers, in Schenectady, working at Schenectady Muni, cutting greens and fairways. It was just after that, during my sophomore year, that I met your mother Diane, who was also going to Florida State. We dated all through school and, unlike you, got married when we were still in school, in our senior year. To this day I regret that I never actually graduated, because I took a job as an assistant pro, instead of going another semester. I always planned on finishing, in fact you might remember that I took some correspondence courses, but I still was nine credit hours short. Ten years later, about when you were in junior high, I finally called the university again to arrange finishing up my degree, but the requirements had changed and it turned out that I needed fifteen more hours, so I said the heck with it. If I were to call now and give them a big donation, I could probably get a diploma!

I had our family to support. Your mom and I were only a month out of school when your brother Brent was born. I had thought about trying to play on the Tour but there wasn't a lot of money on it then, unless you were a star. And it was hard to qualify. Even Hubert missed the first year of qualifying school. He became an assistant pro at Winged Foot, where he did a lot of teaching. His boss was Claude Harmon, whose son, Butch, is now Tiger's coach. A lot of the tour players worked for Harmon senior, who was both a great teacher and a great player—he won the Masters. He hired these guys like Hubert to teach and play with the members. I can't understand why Claude Harmon's not in the Hall of Fame.

I was also an assistant pro, working for Uncle Jim's Florida State classmate Dave Philo at the same private club, Timuquana, in Jacksonville, where we moved back to later, when you were a little girl. What a great old Donald Ross course, but I didn't know it then. I was only twenty-one years old and needed a job. I worked for Philo for one year. We rented a trailer and lived in it for one year in Ware's Trailer Park, west of Jacksonville. That was all in 1968—seems so long ago. We moved into that trailer in the middle of summer. It had no air conditioner. I remember we bought one and I put it in the window and I wired it right to the outside utility pole to get some cool air in that trailer. That was big-time for your mom and me, a major event, having our own air conditioner. And a TV. I remember watching TV on the floor of the trailer when the draft lottery took place, to see who was going to be drafted to Vietnam. My number came up, October 9th; and it was 342 or something like that. I think they drafted up to about 140 or 150. So, no army for me.

Working that first year at Timuquana, I never did get to play much. I was in the shop all the time, selling stuff. Gave a few lessons. Then I got a job at Fernandina Beach, at the old municipal golf course just north of where they would build Amelia Island Plantation. I ended up being on the island for five years; in fact, I was there when Amelia first started. Sea Pines Company had just bought the property. The owner, Charles Frazier, wanted to prevent anyone from strip-mining the land, which would have ruined the whole island. Sea Pines, at Hilton Head, South Carolina, was so successful that Frazier had decided to develop a resort on his new property in Amelia.

We had moved out of the trailer and rented a place on the beach. One hundred and twenty-five dollars a month for the lower level of a duplex. Then we found a nicer place for just a few dollars more. We were in the first place for two years, and then the second place for another year, and then we bought in downtown Fernandina. Man, that was a huge deal for us—twelve thousand, five hundred dollars! When we sold the house two years later for twenty-five thousand dollars, we thought we were rich.

I had a great job there at Fernandina Beach, working for Tommy Birdsong, who was like a father to me. Gave some lessons and played all the time. But then I left to become assistant pro at Charles Frazier's resort, Amelia Island Plantation, under Dutch Hood. I had applied for the head pro job—I had my PGA Class A card by then—

but they brought in Dutch Hood, who was a top pro, and he hired me as his first assistant. This was in 1973. Brent was five, and David—let's see, he was born in 1971, so that made him two years old. You hadn't appeared yet.

We opened the original golf course at Amelia. It was called Marshview—the first nine holes that were opened; then Oyster Bay came second. And that was followed by Oceanside, with those beautiful holes by the beach. They were all designed by Pete Dye, who later became the architect of the TPC stadium course here in Ponte Vedra. He wasn't building island greens back then, but he was already using railroad ties. Mostly his designs at Amelia just had a nice feel to them, like they belonged there, and that's the first place where your brother David ever went out with me onto a golf course. Except he never got to play there—he wasn't old enough—because I only stayed at Amelia for a year.

One day at Amelia, in 1974, I was about to close up when I got a phone call from two Timuquana board members, Jimmy Bent and Del Conley (who was also president of the club). Nice men, they knew me from when I'd worked there after college. I was also playing golf all over the Jacksonville area, winning some local tournaments, so I guess that had kept my name in their minds. I was learning how earlier relationships can have a major impact later on, which is also what happens in golf. Your brother's rivalry with Tiger or Phil Mickelson, for that matter—if rivalry is the right word, I know

David doesn't say it—goes back to their first matches. It's the history of the relationship, in part, that makes it interesting when they play against one another today. Interesting not just for the people who watch, but, though they might deny it, for them, too. But it's a tremendously important factor in golf, something most instructors miss, maybe because they haven't been players, or because they don't know how to respond to this in their teaching. And I'm not putting them down personally when I mention this, just observing it. But it's really a crucial factor.

Your brother wins because he's so long off the tee and has all the shots, even his bunker shots are getting a lot better with all the practice time he's been devoting to them. And a few years ago he really became a great putter. But he also wins because of the way he approaches a match, the way he relates to other people, other golfers, that attitude he has. I don't mean attitude in a bad way, but the basics of how he is in the world.

"It's just a game, Dad," he's always saying. Imagine competing against someone who really, truly believes that—plus he can hit it 40, 50 yards farther than you!

But to get back to my story:

"Dave Philo is leaving Timuquana," Jimmy Bent and Del Conley told me that May day in 1974 on the phone. "Bobby, do you want to be the head pro?"

I was twenty-seven years old. Your grandfather Hap was still working while he tried to take care of your grandmother Anne, who was already very sick with the cancer that would kill her. I didn't hesitate answering, but I didn't want to appear too eager. It's like in a golf tournament—it's okay to feel what you're feeling, but you don't ever want to seem like you can't believe it when you get into the field for a big event.

"Can we talk about it?" I asked.

"Why don't you come down for lunch to Jacksonville?" they said.

So we met at the River Club. They said fine to everything I asked. Dave had to do his own billing, because he owned the golf shop at the club and everything the members bought he had to bill. I wanted guaranteed billing, so I could turn my receipts over to the club and they'd reimburse me, then bill the members for their pro shop purchases. I didn't want to have to go through all that bookkeeping. I did keep the books, but I didn't have to do the mailing. And I was guaranteed to get paid every month, too.

At first, after I became head pro at Timuquana, I commuted from Amelia. It would have been hard to keep doing that, but when we moved to Old Ortega I missed some of my pals. That feeling disappeared instantly after Brent got sick. Now when I think of Old Ortega it's where he lived the last half of his short life. When I go by the house today, on my way to visit the Moores, I think how young you were, just a few years old.

Don't know why I got into all that. I was just going to tell you how it was we ended up where we were, so you would know it, in the order it happened—not the piecemeal of memories and stories and legends we grow up with. But these histories never come out clean. Maybe that's one of the reasons I couldn't imagine being away from golf for very long, like I was last summer after my elbow surgery. As long as it's there, as long as there's some aspect of my game to work on, I've got a focus and purpose, a goal. And then, when I'm playing, even a round that has a hiccup or two, there's still more or less a straight line to it, so to speak—a progression, an order. If only life were that simple.

The club members at Timuquana were always great to me. They wanted me to play golf, too. In fact, they wanted me to try and qualify for the U.S. Open, which would reflect well on the club, the oldest in Jacksonville. I knew I was pretty young to be the head pro. I was on top of the world, I really was! There weren't that many clubs in Jacksonville, and here I was, head pro at Timuquana. My salary doubled, from about $20,000 a year working my ass off to $40,000-plus and having a nice time doing it. Running my own operation. I did a good job there, and they liked me. The club made me an honorary member when I went out on the Senior Tour. Honored to be one.

But the greatest prize was always you.

Much love,
Dad

7

It's all instinct

January 10

Dear Michele,

Hey beautiful, that was sweet of you to drop by. We're still getting used to this new spot. Wish Murray could have been with you, but know he had to work, playing the piano at that reception. I guess this is a busy time of year for a pianist, all the parties and everything. Or is it quieting down some now that the holidays are over?

I'm hoping if Murray has time I can get him out on the golf course again, before I leave for the first tournament. That's in three weeks, the Mastercard Championship, except we'll leave a little early because it's such a long trip to Hawaii. Please tell Murray I want him to work on his short game like he plays the piano. He's so smooth when he performs, never seems to give it a thought no matter what song people ask for, even if it's a song he doesn't know and he has to ask them to hum a little of it for him. I was watching him last time, how he listens for a moment, catches the tune, and then takes off. It's all instinct, no mechanics at all. That's exactly like golf, Michele. I meant to tell him that but then we left before he'd finished and now it's the new year. Shari says Happy New Year. And I do, too—

XO
Bobby

8

Glare at your target, glance at the ball

January 12

Dear Colin,

So we're leaving for Hawaii in a few days and I guess I'm not going to get over to Pablo again before we go. Anyway, just to say if I miss you, stop thinking about all those mechanics when you're on the tee. Pick out your target, do your setup, and get on with it. You remember what I said to you the first time you came for a lesson? When was that, more than twenty years ago? Glare at your target, glance at the ball—then go!

—Your humble pro

9

Stick with the short stuff

January 21

Dear Doc,

Just a postcard to tell you what a terrific time you've been missing here in Kaupulehu. Played great the first round, then lost it a little the second, came back, kind of, in the third. No pain in my elbow, though, just wanted you to know. I was pretty sure it would be okay, after all the rehab. Dr. Andrews and his gang up there in Alabama did a good job. As for you, Rear Admiral Moore, stick with the short stuff—the clubs you use last—when you're practicing if you want to finish off those par fives with some birdie putts. Put your motto to work on the golf course: "Give your end a new beginning." That was pretty funny when I came in with those hemorrhoids. If I were you, I wouldn't even hit a long iron or wood; sure, it's nice to be in the fairway, but your score isn't the total of fairways hit. Larry Nelson won this tournament here, and he's got some distance he didn't used to have, but you should see him with a wedge. When we finish the dock I'm going to have a mat there so I can hit wedges across the Intercoastal. No one gets dinner until he hits the bucket by the palm tree—

BD

10
"Play the ball down"

February 2

Dear Jimmy,

Ouch—tied for 32nd today in the Royal Caribbean. Forgotten what happens when you don't play for a long time—I mean really play, not just play around. But it's nice down here in Miami. Shari's with me, and I'm back for another tournament. If I never win another one I already know what I accomplished. Sometimes I get into a conversation with one of the guys about what took me so long to get here—you know, why didn't I play the regular tour when I was younger? They mean the question as a compliment, I believe, but I can truly say I never ask it to myself, and not because I never wondered.

First of all, I know the answer, and for all the things we went through as a family—mine, not ours growing up—all the heartache, I would never have done something else, been someone else. We are who we are. You can't play golf pretending you're someone else, and you sure can't live your life that way. "We play the ball down," can't you just here Dad saying that to us? But he was right, and not just about the rules of golf, the breaks of the game. The struggle, all the effort to learn and prepare, and then the seeming ease when it comes—that is the game.

And then, if you're in a divot, or behind a tree (like I was a few times today!), you play the shot. I can never figure out people who want to change a lie, take a free drop, pretend they don't know the stroke-and-distance rule when they've just gone out of bounds. I don't mean guys out here, though you hear an occasional story, but no one lasts very long. But just the average player, whatever their skill level. There's no rule I'm aware of that says that above such and such a handicap the rules don't apply. Isn't that what makes it golf?

How'd I get started on that? I meant to tell you about the iguanas they have here. There was one on the 12th hole, a par three that must have been 5 or 6 feet long.

I'll call later,
Bobby

11
Deal with your fears before you play

March 6

Dear John,

I think you're being too hard on yourself. Not to make things too neat, nor to confuse golf and life—they are closely related for anyone who plays, though they are not the same thing. But it is a certainty in golf that recovery from loss (poor shots, bad swings, lost matches, or what I think you're feeling, a loss of the very confidence that has made you a success in your profession) is the single most necessary attribute for the success in golf I know you so badly want. Remember, even Tiger with his amazing record still loses many more tournaments than he wins. So the first thing you can do, right now, to make yourself a golfer is to work on your attitude. And you can do that anywhere, in the shower, on your way to the office, in the middle of a meeting. . . . You don't need a club in your hand, in fact that will only get in your way (as it so often does on the course!). Try visualizing yourself making good swings; see the ball land where you imagined it was going; watch pretend putts drop into the hole. It may sound corny but you'd be amazed how it can become habit-forming. Kind of the golfing version of smile and the world smiles with you.

Speaking of Tiger and attitude, I know he took some hits when he first burst onto the scene in 1996—can it really be that recently?—and he'd do that thing with his arms they started calling the Tiger pump. And there were people who criticized him for it, as if no one else had ever showed emotion on the golf course. Well, I've never played with Tiger, but I remember the next year, 1997—when David won his first tournaments—and the two of them played in November at the Skins Game. Mark O'Meara and Tom Lehman were the other players, if I remember, and David had been included at the last minute as a replacement for Fred Couples, whose father was very ill. So you-know-who did caddy duty again. And I had just completed my first year on the Senior Tour.

While the guys were warming up on the range, Tiger came over and introduced himself.

"How do you do, Mr. Duval," he said. "Congratulations on the great season you just had on the Senior Tour."

That impressed me; here was this young man who had just won the first Masters in which he competed as a pro. Of course, it was pretty impressive to see him swing the golf club, too—never seen anyone drive it that far.

Yes, you also have to have the shots, maybe not like Tiger, but you want to know what the different clubs can do and be able to hit them. And there's always a new shot to learn. That's what makes the game fun. But even when you're actually playing for something—a beer, a match, your career—the most important part of your game is going to be taking whatever it is you can already do when you're just hitting balls and pulling it off for real. It sounds so simple, and in some ways it is. But then you've got a one-foot putt to win the Masters like Scott Hoch did several years ago, or a soft nine-iron to the last green like Greg Norman did in the 1993 Tour Championship at the Olympic Club in San Francisco, and suddenly that little putt or that short nine-iron makes you feel like you're walking a tightrope high above the crowd under the bigtop, or landing a jet on a moving aircraft carrier, or going over Niagara Falls in a barrel. I know this feeling, which is why I have such respect for Scott and Greg—they've dealt with it and gone on, the hardest thing in golf, much more difficult than any particular shot.

Two years before my victory at the Emerald Coast Classic, I finished second at a tournament in Pittsburgh—when I was leading by four strokes with only six holes to play. I ended up in a playoff, which I lost to my South African friend Hugh Baiocchi on the sixth playoff hole. That was a big disappointment to get over; the next year in the very same tournament in Pittsburgh I finished second again. I wanted that victory too badly, I guess. Last week in California, I couldn't putt. In fact, I've been putting pretty mediocre most of this season. So I'm writing you, John, but I'm talking to myself, too.

When you're playing golf, whether you're a beginner or a pro, the prospect of disaster lurks before every shot. Possibly, John, you will be faced with a situation you don't know how to handle technically—a shot over water, say, with a strong headwind to a green with a pin tucked up front. You do your best at such moments, but if you don't pull off the shot or devise a strategy to avoid it, you move on. Later, you can practice the shot or have someone teach it to you for the next time. More likely the potential trouble, the dangerous kind that ruins a great round or an entire tournament, will be invisible. Instead of being a hazard on the golf course it will be something inside your head: a persistent voice you can't quiet, an image that won't go away. You become scared, lose your focus, forget your routine, project results—and the worst, the very thing you fear, happens. From the middle of the fairway, with a perfect lie, you shank your ball into a bunker that shouldn't even have been in play. On the green in regulation you blow your first putt past the hole, miss the comebacker, angrily begin to tap in the third and, instead, you whiff. The group on the tee at the next hole is talking loudly and you let their chatter distract you in the middle of your backswing: that's out of bounds over there?

To make shots that count—for me, in a tournament, for you, when you first play a real round—you have to deal with your anxieties before you play. You have to prepare emotionally, mentally, psychologically the same way you work out, eat well, get enough sleep, take care of the rest of your life—before you arrive at the golf course. I used to think the equation worked the other way. If you could only pull "it" off—win the Masters, beat the champion—then you could deal with whatever it is inside yourself that had kept you until then from achieving your own personal version of the impossible. It took me most of my adult lifetime to realize I had this backward. I had to learn what it feels like to succeed, in fact I suppose you could say, as far as my golf goes, that's what I was doing all those years while I was a club pro giving lessons and playing in local tournaments when I could. Or times like the day someone in Tallahassee called and said there was someone in town who was looking for a match with a guy who could play, he had a lot of money to stake himself, and so I went and cleaned him out. But it could have ended the other way, and sometimes, earlier in my life, it did.

You learn to do that just like you learn to swing your driver. Or anything else in your game—or your life. It's not magic but a matter of prior effort, and then repetition. The magic feeling, the sense of ease, comes afterward. The challenge is to make this feeling a part of you.

It's so great you want to get out there. That's the first step. Take it!

Yours,
Bob Duval

12
"When are you going to do it?"

March 26

Dear Jeremy,

Well, that was more like it. Even-par 70 each day, 15th place, and not a bad check. I always seem to play good here in Pensacola. Funny how that goes, but I had a feeling things would turn around this week in the Emerald Coast, and they did. You know how hard I'd been working on the short game, man, I was logging more hours on the putting green than you and I used to in the pro shop back at the Plantation. And we put our time in there, yes sir.

Did you catch any of David's commentary at the Players Championship? He seemed like himself, relaxed, smiling, funny. Not at all sorry for himself that he couldn't play. I just hope that wrist heals with the Masters only two weeks away.

We're not going up to Augusta this year. My elbow's okay but I'm beginning to sense a soreness in my left shoulder. Maybe it's a residue of the rehab I did last fall after the elbow surgery, but I'm afraid it may be something else, maybe something that's been building for a long time and suddenly I'm noticing it now, especially on full shots. And you can't play golf like that, protecting against a particular pain or malady. You start protecting and eventually your whole game comes apart. It's like someone whose business has a weak point. You can do some fancy accounting to make it seem okay for a while, but it's going to catch up with you finally. "Deal with it," my dad Hap used to say.

I remember when David first came out on Tour and had all those seconds, people were beginning to question if he had the game to win—not the physical game but the inner stuff to use that game, all that talent, when he had to. And he couldn't hide from it. That's the brutal thing about golf. If the scorecard says you finished second then you finished second. If this keeps happening and you know deep down you could be winning, I mean you know you have the game—David sure did, sure does—then you deal with it.

"Dad," he used to say to me back before I turned fifty. "When are you going to stop talking about how you could be playing on the Senior Tour? When are you going to do it?"

That was a hard time, I don't have to remind you, because you were there with me. Nice golf course, wealthy members, I was set for as long as I stayed, and I could have stayed until I retired. But I wasn't happy. David was out on his own; Deirdre was starting college. With the divorce I was pretty well cleaned out money-wise. The smart thing, the secure thing, was to hold onto that job at the Plantation, or even look for another one like it and get myself back on my feet financially and then start planning for the future, for the day I couldn't work, and somewhere in there of course, as you also know, I was getting remarried. And where were we going to live? What were we going to live on? How was I going to support my new wife?

"No boyfriend, girlfriend stuff for me," Shari said. "We do this right or we're not doing it."

We did it right.

"Play to your strengths," was another thing Hap taught me. And he didn't mean just the kind of shots you used in the clutch. He meant—at least this is what I think he meant—that when you're faced with a big decision, you should go back to what you do best, rely on that, build from it.

Trust it.

The center of yourself.

When I was a boy playing at my dad's Stanford course my life was pretty much focused exclusively on golf by the time I was ten or eleven years old. Even during the school year I used to go over to the golf course as much as I could. And because Schenectady gets cold during many months of the year I had to learn at an early age how to play golf under all sorts of conditions.

More than forty years later I remember that course

and my routine there so well. I can see the second hole in my mind—it was short enough to drive the green. I remember how, during the summer, we used to stop for snacks at the farm stand near the fourth green. Because I played so often, most of the regulars knew me, and I was soon playing golf with people several years older than I. Don't remember exactly when I had my growth spurt—in my height, in my game—but in team events, I was often paired with someone almost as old as my father.

Because Stanford was privately run the owner could do what he wanted with it. And so, unfortunately, he sold it to a developer who then built a shopping center called the Mohawk Mall, which is now defunct. My dad had to find another golf course to work at, and, it turned out, I had to find another one to play at because my dad's new course was too far away from our house for me to get to on my bike. That's when I started playing a lot at Schenectady Muni. During the fall, because I didn't play football, I'd ride my bike over to the golf course after school and play until dark. By late October and into early November, before the first snows came, the course was usually pretty empty in the afternoons when I got there. In fact, because of the change from daylight saving time, I often found myself playing alone.

The wind used to blow pretty good in Schenectady. I'd be wearing my school pants, sneakers, a long-sleeved shirt, a sweater, and a jacket. I never liked to wear a hat. I usually played a couple of balls, sometimes practicing a solitary game in which, after hitting both balls, I would then walk to the ball that was in the worst position and play my next two shots from there. Then, again, I'd walk to the ball that was now in the worst position, and again play both balls from there. I'd repeat this process until I holed out. It was a great discipline, mentally and physically, because I had to learn how to hit awkward shots, and because it also developed patience and dedication.

I loved the feeling of being out on the golf course, loved the sensation that ran through your whole body when you made a good shot, the tingle in your forearms when you hit one flush, the feeling of the hard, frozen ground underfoot in very late fall, maybe even snow flakes melting on your face just before Thanksgiving. I loved to hear the wind blow the leaves in the woods. I loved looking at the gray Schenectady sky. Sometimes I would stop somewhere on the course, a bunker near one of the greens on the back nine, and I'd practice bunker shots, using all the old golf balls I carried in the storage compartment of my canvas golf bag. I saved the good balls for weekends—if my dad hadn't given me some, the only ones I could afford were called Club Specials. They were made by the Acushnet company, which is the same company that owns Titleist, one of my sponsors today. Me, a Club Special, and nobody on the next tee—sounds pretty perfect, doesn't it?

Give me a call and we'll get up a game–

Pro

13 The circumstance of the moment

April 1

Dear Scottie,

Know you'll be there at Augusta rooting for David. But since we won't be able to thought I'd write you something that's been on my mind since the last time I talked with your dad. With all the traveling you do in your job you don't get to play as much as you'd like, so when you do you want to get the most you can out of your round. You don't want to be one of those golfers who comes home, and when someone in their family asks them how it was they say, "Lousy." Why would anyone want to spend several hours of his or her time, not to mention the expense, and have a lousy time? Doesn't make much sense, does it?

For me at least, the circumstance of the moment is what I always find myself up against if things aren't going just the way I had hoped they would. Instead of the routine you've been following all your life, suddenly you start wondering about who you're playing with, what the score is, why your ball is sitting down in a ditch, what you just overheard someone in the gallery say. I keep remembering what David told me before the last round of my Emerald Coast victory—how you can't control what anyone else does, you can only control what *you* do. So, you just think about hitting each shot the way you would on the range, and if someone else plays better than you, so what?

Of course, part of the deal is learning how to accept things when they are not going your way. But that's not the same thing as forgetting. What's crucial, it seems to me, is to be realistic about what you're doing—how your round is going, what kind of shots you can and can't play, what your overall goals are. For me, just to be playing out on the Senior Tour with people I used to watch on television is exciting.

Your dad probably never shared much of this with you, but back in the mid '90s, when I left my position as head professional at the Plantation Country Club, after David had been after me to give the Senior Tour a real shot, I wound up at first doing a little teaching at one of the places where I had started my career—Amelia Island Plantation. I was still afraid to make the big move.

"Bobby, let's figure out if you really want to do this," Shari said to me one day. I'd been practicing hard and the lessons were bringing in some much-needed cash, but I knew the answer.

"I want to play," I said. And I did. Wanted it more than I realized, since the days when my kids were growing up. You remember when you used to visit, back before Brent died? You were the same age. I know you still think about him a lot. Your dad told me that just the other day you said on the phone, "I wonder what Brent would be doing now?"

Raising a family. Playing a little golf. Going to the Masters with you.

Shari and I were married in 1996, when I entered a club pro series of tournaments to work a little on my game. At one of the tournaments, someone told me that Jack Nicklaus was starting a satellite circuit called the Golden Bear Tour in southern Florida. The entry fee was $15,000 upfront, and this entitled you to play in fourteen tournaments. You also had to live down in southern Florida while you were competing.

Fifteen thousand was a lot of money to me then—I was basically broke—but I put a deposit down to reserve a spot in this new tour. Then Shari got together a proposal for people interested in investing in my new career as a player. Six of my close friends ended up contributing $5,000 each, money I would have to pay back if and when I started making a profit as a player.

Shari and I headed down south toward Miami and I began playing in the Golden Bear tournaments, usually against golfers half my age, in fact many of them were guys David had played against in college, so they were calling me Mr. Duval. One week I finished 10th, another week 11th. Then I won an event and began to sense that I could do this. All told, I made more than $29,000, just enough to pay back each of the partners' investments. One of them offered to renew the deal, but after Shari and I talked it over we told him, "Thank you, that's very generous, but we're going to try to do this now on our own ticket."

So we headed off to California, where I played in the Transamerica Classic, a Senior Tour event, held at Silverado in Napa Valley. IMG, the big agency, gave me a sponsors' exemption. I played okay; the highlight was a birdie on the first hole. But the best thing about playing in that tournament at Napa was that David caddied for me. Although his being there made me more nervous than the actual playing, I was a very proud father. That might have been the first time a caddy was introduced on the first tee. When we finished the round everyone was asking for David's autograph, not mine.

"Hey, David," I said. "Who's the player here?"

Before I came home I qualified for another Senior Tour event by finishing first in a six-way playoff for the one spot. I made about $12,000, and that was all the money in the world to me, literally. I'd already spent what little I had on the Golden Bear Tour and living expenses because I'd given up my regular income from Plantation when I resigned.

David also caddied for me later that fall in St. Augustine, Florida, during the first stage of Senior Tour qualifying—Q-School. I finished third. Shari and our friend Michele—you've met her, she's married to Murray, the pianist who went to Princeton and used to be in the real estate business—were my gallery.

"I wonder where Shari and Michele are," I said to David at one point during one of the rounds.

"Forget them," said David. "You're not out here to socialize. You're playing in a golf tournament, Dad."

That moment was certainly a new experience for me. The father-son role had been totally reversed.

Remember, Scottie, it's still 1996—all this happened in the same incredible year. The next and final stage of Senior Tour qualifying was four rounds at the Valley Course at the Tournament Players Club in Ponte Vedra, near where we now live. On the first day I played okay, and then improved a little on the second. My third round was really good, putting me in position to get one of the coveted places to play on the following years' Senior Tour. There were just sixteen spots; eight of the contestants would have a full exemption, and the next eight provisional. The situation was kind of a closed shop for those who hadn't played the regular Tour and could therefore qualify on their lifetime earnings.

Play what's in front of you, I said to myself. No way I was going to be able to change the regulations myself. *Deal with them,* I could hear an inner voice telling me.

I remember it was very cold and windy the morning

of the fourth and final round. I stood at a couple over par when I reached the 14th hole, a little par three, where I made a 20-footer for birdie.

"Now," I said to myself, "this is the final four holes of the qualifying school. Focus. Do what you know you can do."

For a few holes, I did. On the 15th hole I had a good drive, followed by a good three-iron to the green. Made par. On the 16th hole I hit an iron into the green and made a birdie, too. On the 17th, another par five, I overheard one of my friends say, "You're going to make it." And, instead, I half topped my second shot, a three-wood, and it flew off the green, but I was able to save par from there—I hit a wedge so good that it hit the flag and spun back to the front of the green. Two-putted for par. The last hole I hit a really good drive and had about 200 yards to the flag, into the wind.

"Give me a four-iron," I said to my caddie. It was a shot I'd hit countless times in my life. But I got ahead of myself. I was a little quick, the wind took the ball, and I saw it splash in the pond adjacent to the green.

"Now I've blown it," I said to myself. "What in the heck am I going to do now?" I took my penalty drop, focused, and chipped to five feet from the hole. I made the bogey putt. I felt terrible—I was actually crying because I was sure that the one-shot penalty I'd incurred for making the mistake of hitting that four-iron into the pond was going to keep me from getting my Senior Tour card.

But, amazingly, when everyone was finished playing, four of us were tied for what would be the 15th and 16th spots. So, it was back to the golf course, and I hit a two-iron off the tee of the first playoff hole, a par five. I followed that shot with a three-iron and then a wedge, which left my ball touching a rake next to a bunker.

A rules official told me I could move the rake, but not the ball. I chipped to four feet and made the putt for par, as did two of the other people competing against me. The fourth man made a bogey, which meant he was now out of the playoff.

There was no talking, no joking. Everyone was very serious. On the next playoff hole, a par three, I hit a seven-iron to 7 feet. What happened after that I don't remember; I do know I made the putt to birdie the hole. The other two players made par, which meant the playoff continued for them, but I was in.

"I've got my card!" I said to myself. I couldn't believe it. A good friend of mine, Chris Blocker, had been carrying a bottle of champagne all during the round. As I came off the green he opened it and sprayed it all over me. Later, I joined the other fifteen players who had made it through Q-School at a reception. The very next morning, I played in a pro-am in Gainesville, where I finished in the top five. I was flying.

But even with my new status I couldn't get into the field for any of the early tournaments held at the beginning of the '97 Senior Tour season in Florida, so I had to qualify or seek sponsor exemptions to play in them. I won $5,000 in one of them, which meant that I had enough money to keep playing the next week. Then, I don't know quite what happened, but I stopped worrying and started really playing. I finished second to Gil Morgan in a tournament and won more money than I had ever received for doing anything in my entire professional life. Soon after that, another second-place finish earned me $96,000. Titleist had already offered me a small deal for using their equipment when I was on the Golden Bear Tour; after I got my card, they gave me a really nice one. Tommy Hilfiger did the same. Against all odds, I ended up 28th on the money list among the seniors for the season. This meant that I was fully exempt for the following year's Senior Tour. I was on my way, with no more Monday qualifiers. That next year, 1998, I finished in seventeenth place, and then in '99 I was 24th overall.

I guess the moral of this story is to believe in yourself and give whatever it is you dream of a chance. It seems like that's what you've been doing in your work at Coca-Cola, the way you're constantly traveling, but you've got your feet on the ground, just like your brother Ben with his acting at college. I share your parents' pride.

Come see us sometime; we'll tee it up together.

Love,
Uncle Bobby

14

Put the bag on your shoulder

April 16

Dear John,

You're right, that was some Masters. How close David came. I didn't realize until I got your message that this was the first golf telecast you had watched. You picked a good one to start with. Yes, you're right, they hit it far. How do you create such power? That's one of the great mysteries of the game. I remember when David was a kid, hanging out at Timuquana, and he was already good enough to play with some of our best members. He could putt and he had a developing short game, hit his irons great, but his best drives didn't go any farther than an old man's. Of course, he was only eleven or twelve years old. Little by little his length developed, but it was nothing you would have particularly noticed. Then, when he was around fourteen, I think it was after school got out that year and he was playing every day, suddenly he was blowing it by everybody. A year later, I went out with him one night after I'd finished teaching and we played nine holes. On just about every par four and par five he outdrove me.

I'll tell you one thing about power: You don't create it from a perfect grip or a perfect swing. There is no such thing, John. It's different for each person. Think of the swing as a circular motion that you're making around your body, so it's like your body is a top and you're spinning. Another thing: always remember you're not trying to hit the golf ball. You're trying to move it somewhere—to your target. We'll work on some mechanics when we get together, but right now I wouldn't worry about how far the ball is going. Like I always tell people, if you want to learn how to play golf, put the bag over your shoulder and play. Keep doing that; keep your target in mind, and the rest will come.

Yours,
Bob

P.S. You're right, too, about concentration, although I don't imagine it's any different for you in your profession or anyone for that matter who's really doing their job. I heard a story about a man cutting trees adjacent to Riviera Country Club in Los Angeles, where the Nissan/LA Open on the PGA Tour is played every February. It's a famous golf course—Hogan's Alley, people still call it, for the consecutive Los Angeles Opens that Ben Hogan won there, and the U.S. Open he captured in 1948, also at Riviera.

Hogan was renowned for many things—his practice ethic, his steely-eyed presence on the golf course, his comeback from a near-fatal automobile accident. The accident took place in 1949, and there were doubts he would ever walk again. Instead, he returned to the tour in 1950, and the first tournament he played was at Riviera. Amazingly, he almost won there again, losing in a playoff to Sam Snead.

I don't know what someone was doing cutting trees at Riviera during the tournament in 1998, but he was causing quite a racket. No one could figure out how to stop it, because he wasn't on the course property. Anyway, one of the golfers who was playing then in the tournament was asked afterward how much the sound of the chainsaw had bothered him and he asked, "What chainsaw?"

It's a true story. I know, because the golfer was my son David. But I would have known it was true anyway. Too bad you weren't into golf a few years ago when David shot 59 in the final round to win the only PGA Tour event still named after an entertainer—Bob Hope, who in his nineties annually shows up for the tournament from his home there in Palm Springs. So, on that Sunday afternoon in Palm Springs, California, in front of David was an expanse of fairway and water and an eighteenth flagstick 226 yards away. Before a large gallery and with millions of people watching on national television, he hit a five-iron over water to a spot below a ridge on the green, where the ball bounced up and ran forward, toward the hole, stopping about 12 feet from it. Can you imagine the concentration that took? There was no way he didn't already know his score as he lined up that putt. That five-iron over the water was his fifty-eighth stroke, and he made the putt for his historic 59.

Of course, when you're playing you're probably never going to try and pull off a long five-iron to a distant green, whatever your score is. It's like the day we were playing over at Pablo, me and Colin versus David and another friend, and on one of the long holes on the front nine David had 240 yards to the pin after his drive. And the wind was in our face. So he hits a two-iron, starts it out left of the target and cuts it back right, toward the flagstick. Hits it stiff.

"Nice shot," one of the other guys in our group says to him.

"Thank you," says David, smiling. "That's a shot you'll never hit."

He wasn't boasting when he said it. It was just the truth. There might be ten guys on Tour who can hit a 240-yard cut-shot into the wind.

15
Cheer me up

April 22

Dear Colin,

Good thing you didn't bother to come out here to Las Vegas; I sandwiched two good scores around a very nasty 78. And I wish I could wonder when I last shot a score like that, but I know the answer—a few weeks ago in Silicon Valley. So there wouldn't have been much for you to cheer for, though you could have helped me cheer up. It's my left shoulder, I'm sure of that now; it's getting worse each time I play.

Sometimes in the locker room out here it seems like the only thing the guys talk about is their health.

"Going in for my MRI next week," someone will say.

"Not me. Sticking with the Celebrex, see if that does the trick."

It's not exactly inspirational, I'll tell you that. You know, we're well paid entertainers, and it's pretty neat to get paid for doing this, but after shooting 78 on national television with your shoulder hurting you can feel pretty lonely here in Las Vegas.

I think our flight into Birmingham gets us there by the late afternoon. I'll leave you a clubhouse pass at the Will Call gate if you can make it, which would be great.

—BD

16
Not afraid to go low

April 29

Hello Hubert,

Thought you were going to run the table there in Birmingham after that opening 67. Nice tournament, though. It's amazing to me, now that I've been out here a while, to realize how fine the margins are; you followed that 67 with, what was it, a 70? And then closed with a 74 for 28th place; I had my bad round first, a 75, but then I came back with a 69 and 70, the second week in a row I've had two good rounds out of the usual three that we play. Anyway, the one-stroke difference of my 75 and your 74, and the two-stroke margin of your 67 and my 69, when you combine it with the 70 we each shot in our other round, put me a tie for 47th—three strokes total, but a difference of almost twenty places from you. Not like it was back at Florida State, when we used to play together on the same team, and there would be tournaments when some of the schools we competed against didn't have a player who could consistently break 80.

You know I never emphasize score when I'm giving a clinic or talking with the guys in my pro-am group at a tournament, but I wonder what the average golfer understands about score. With all the equipment that beginners buy, and the constant reading of books and magazines, and all those hours watching the Golf Channel, do they remember that the object of the game is to put the ball in the hole? Not to make the prettiest swing. Not to have the fanciest equipment.

To put the ball in the hole.

One of the friends I play with when I'm home, an Englishman named Colin, started taking lessons with me when I was still the pro at Timuquana. We've known each other more than twenty years. Colin's the kind of amateur golfer who might have a bad hole now and then, even a bad round, but he's got a good game, gets it off the tee 230 or more yards, and likes to compete. He'll never have our game, nor does he expect to; he's done that in business. But the thing about him that reminds me a little of you is he's not afraid of shooting a good score. He's not afraid of going low.

Enjoy your time off. If this shoulder hasn't fallen off by then I'll see you in New Jersey at the Senior PGA.

—Bobby

17
The margins are so thin

May 3

Dear John,

You're right, we do move around a lot—last week in Birmingham, this week in Charlotte. It's in the nature of our work, but there's also something about the game that gets you places, too—maybe not like this, with flights to take, hotels to check into (Shari and I always like the ones that comes with a kitchenette, because we don't have to eat in a restaurant every night), new people to meet. But every round of golf, even at the same course, is different, and you'll find that once you've been playing some you'll want to explore other courses besides the one where you're going to be taking lessons. Those lessons must be starting soon—yes?—now that the warm weather has returned to your neck of the woods.

On the Senior Tour, when we get to another course, the first thing I think about is my strategy for the week—

how I'm going to manage the particular course. If I haven't played it before, I will try to get a sense of its style from what I know about the architect, because each architect has his idiosyncrasies. Some courses seem designed for a certain kind of player; the place we go to in Long Island, for example, is a hooker's golf course—many of the holes set up so your drive or approach, or both, call for a right to left shot. Other courses require high approaches, because the greens are well guarded. You have to assess the kind of greens a golf course has, too—not just their size, shape, and contour, but how receptive they are to a ball that comes in high, or one that wants to check up with a lot of backspin. On almost every golf course there is at least one hole I don't like, though on the Scottish links courses and the old, classic courses of the northeast I am so enthralled by the beauty, so soothed by the tranquility, that I hardly notice a quirk. The first hole at Turnberry, for example, isn't much—a three-wood off the tee, a nine-iron into the green—but the history and aura of the place dispel any misgivings you may have, and if the wind is howling that nine-iron might be a four- or a five-iron. Not to mention the rough, which is so thick you sometimes can't find your ball, and once you do you're lucky to hack it out; I'm sure doing so is how I hurt my neck back in 1977 when I tried to qualify for the British Open.

To finish answering your question: Another thing about traveling is how it tests your golf. Remember when we talked the time you called me at home, and I mentioned being over at the range? You were asking why people who could already play spent so much time practicing. And I explained that the "elbowroom" is so small out here—the difference between winning and losing—that just one particular shot during a three-day tournament can be the difference between winning and losing, cashing a good check or, in a tournament like the Senior PGA, not even making the cut. And it's not just the numerical significance of one shot—one stroke in your score—but how that shot relates to what preceded and followed it, how it effects the strategy of playing a particular hole, the impact of its result on your psychology and on the other people in your group—so many things.

By the way, I'm stunned when a golfer in a pro-am doesn't assess himself the proper penalty in situations—such as a lost ball off the tee. Instead of going back to the tee, where he'd played the wrong club to begin with, probably causing him to hit the shot that he lost in the woods, he says he'll just take a drop from the woods, like he was doing everyone else a favor, and he might even be a loudmouth about how he's taking his penalty stroke. The correct penalty is stroke and distance, but he has also missed the whole point of the situation he was in to begin with. Seeing the woods from the tee, he should probably never have hit driver, because of the risk of an errant shot. Instead, if he had properly calculated his risks and rewards, with the full knowledge that hitting into the woods and losing his ball would cost him stroke and distance, he should probably have played an iron or fairway wood instead off the tee. This kind of decision making happens all the time on a good golf course and is a crucial part of what makes the game not only interesting but challenging to players of all ability levels.

But the real significance of moving around, whether from your home course to your buddy's or from the Home Depot Invitational here in Charlotte to the Ridgewood Country Club in New Jersey, is the way it removes your game from any of the crutches you've become accustomed to where you usually play—knowing you can't reach the fairway bunker from the first tee, seeing the way the green slopes on the fourth. It exposes your game, so to speak, in all its glory or frailty. On a day-to-day basis that is also a little like what happens when anyone, pro or amateur, takes his or her golf from the range to the course. On the range, for example, I can hit that two-iron cutshot I told you about that David pulled off one day at the TPC. But I've never tried the shot in a match. Actually, when I'm playing on the Senior Tour I don't even carry a two-iron, usually (in fact, lately, I've been using one of these new utility woods, the ones with the small head; I call it my Kmart club, but please don't tell anyone I picked up the one I'm using in the bargain bin in a mall on the road this spring). There are many days out here when I'll play a great "game" on the range, everything firing perfect and I can't wait to get going for real. Then, perhaps a little pumped up when I get to the first tee, I'll pull my drive into some woods or the rough. Or maybe I'll hit the ball a little thin, and instead of taking the trajectory I intended it squirts off into a fairway bunker. So many things can happen, and suddenly, on a day I thought I was going to conquer the world, I'm working to salvage a par.

"The game begins when they hand you the scorecard and the pencil on the first tee," my father Hap used to say. So true, so true. What you're doing really counts now.

Something happened yesterday after the pro-am that put what we've been talking about in a fresh light. It was around 5 p.m. and the course was empty when a few of us decided to play nine more holes. As we were getting set to go a guy who'd been in the gallery that afternoon saw us in the tee and introduced himself, said he was a big golf fan and was there anything he could do, like maybe join us?

"Sure," J.J.—John Jacobs—said. "Join us! My caddy went home for the day. You can ride along with me."

So this fellow rode, watched us play, held the flagstick when someone had a long putt, cheered when J.J. or Gary McCord or John Schroeder made a good shot. We got pretty boisterous—there was a little money on the line—but this only seemed to add to our new friend's enjoyment.

"McCord, you couldn't make a putt as long as your moustache," I shouted.

"Hey, Doo-val, is that a golf shirt you're wearing or a picture of the pizza you had for dinner last night?"

When someone hit a good shot we insulted him. We talked loudly when the outcome of a hole was on the line with a putt. McCord told some terrible jokes, and I said we'd report him to the membership committee at Augusta National, which had barred him from announcing at telecasts of the Masters after he said their greens were treated with bikini wax. I'm sure the people who lived on the golf course could hear us, and they probably thought some teenagers had sneaked onto the course after a party.

Today, when I got back to the locker room, there was a note for me in my locker, and it was addressed to, "Mr. Duval."

"Hey, Gary," I said. "Looks like the commissioner is wise to your act. Did you get one of these warnings, too, for conduct unbecoming a professional?"

But when I opened the envelope I saw that it was a note from the man who had ridden along with us.

"I just wanted to thank you," his note began. "I never enjoyed myself more."

Getting that note made me realize that while we were fooling around yesterday this man had been living out a fantasy. It was almost sad in a way, to think how much witnessing our ridiculous behavior had meant to him. Whatever you do in life, I guess it's easy to become complacent, to take things as they are for granted. That's another discovery you're going to make in golf, how quickly everything can unravel as soon as you start thinking you've got the game licked. I think it's okay to let off some steam now and then, but don't go believing you're any different from the guy you were before you figured out the secret of success in golf.

There is no such secret—that's the secret.

Take care,
Bob

P.S. I appreciate your kindness in mentioning that article you read about my son. It continues to sadden me, what people who have never met David or me or anyone else in our family will sometimes write, as if they had known us intimately for years. Your sensitivity about this means a lot.

After Brent died, we were lost as a family. For a time, my wife kept his room exactly as it had been before he died. The disease Brent had was aplastic anemia, which I had never even heard of until his doctor first explained it. Aplastic anemia, I learned, is an insidious disease in which the body's ability to produce white blood cells mysteriously stops. To try and cure it, Brent underwent a bone marrow transplant at a hospital in Cleveland. David was the donor. The procedure, in which a huge needle is inserted into your hip to draw out the bone marrow, could only be described as a terribly painful experience, physically and psychologically. At first the operation was a success. Then Brent's body began to reject the marrow from his brother, and it seemed like his whole system shut down after that. When he died, less than four months after his diagnosis, without ever returning home once he was admitted to the hospital in Cleveland, I think his brother almost felt responsible. I did, too. I had just turned thirty-five, with everything to live for and a seemingly bright future, and then out of nowhere our oldest child became sick and died, and I had been helpless to do anything. I had to watch him die. Then, devastated beyond the meaning of the word, I still had two kids to raise, a wife who was also trying to cope with our loss, and a job teaching golf where I was supposed to be in a continuous good mood.

I looked for that mood in a bottle, and when I couldn't find it there I left my family for a time and looked for some solace in the company of people who didn't know what had happened to us, to me, to my family. Eventually I came home, but it was to the same emptiness. Every day I would get up and say to myself, "Now, it will be better." But it wasn't. Reminders of Brent were everywhere, and the slightest suggestion of his life—a model plane he'd made, a song he'd loved—could immediately trigger a recollection of the entire tragedy, so overwhelming in its pain and hurt that it seemed physical. My hair was turning gray, there were hollows around my eyes, I lost weight, lost my smile. If I was going to be any help to the people who needed me, I needed to take care of myself, too. One day I finally found the courage to leave, to give those whom I loved the space we all needed to go on with our lives, that I needed to find myself again, so I could still be a good father to the son and daughter, now almost grown, I had left. Next to saying goodbye to Brent that was the hardest thing I ever did.

Only afterward, when I was caddying for David in one of the many golf tournaments he played during college, did I begin to rediscover a joy in life that I thought I had lost forever. That happiness grew ever so tentatively at first and then, at long last, took hold firmly and certainly when I learned to love again, without fear that what I felt, what I knew, would disappear. That's another story, not one I can adequately tell here, but in everything, John—everything at least that matters—there is no halfway. You can't hold back, in other words. In golf, too, as I witnessed inside those ropes, caddying for David, and saw with more than simply a father's pride that he was playing the game without fear of consequences. It's true, as people have pointed out, that we have different personalities, he and I, though I don't know anyone with his sense of humor, his wit. And what a competitor. Imagine, before I played in a single Senior Tour event I had already been pushed to the limits on the golf course by my own son. Anyway, watch him and you'll see what I'm really talking about. Watch him let go!

18

If I could only take what I was doing on the range

May 24

Dear John,

I completely understand, and the way I'm playing you didn't miss much. Better days ahead for both of us! But it would have been nice to meet you, finally, and I could have introduced you to one of my playing partners, Hugh Baiocchi, who had a good round and whose elegant wife walked the whole round with us. Can I take a raincheck on that dinner invitation?

The club here is a classic. Reminds me of some of the old courses I knew when I was growing up, though we would never have had the money to be members. They had it set up at just over 6,900 yards, which should have been to my advantage, with my length. I played the first two holes in even par, with a nice putt to save par on the par-five second. Then I drove it in the rough on number three, my layup was short and so was my chip; I just missed the par putt. One over after three.

It was a spring day, the leaves out in all the tall, old trees that line the fairways. The sun felt good on my face. It was cool enough in the shade that when a breeze blew you felt goosebumps. Then, back in the sun, it was warm. It was like you went from spring to summer, then back to spring, then back to summer, all within a few minutes. I could feel that infinite sense of possibility you can get on the golf course, particularly one as beautiful as Ridgewood.

After I got back to even par with a birdie three on number seven (sank a 15-footer), and almost birdied the par-three eighth, a nifty downhill hole just over 200 yards in length, my game seemed to be in sync with my feelings. Big mistake, thinking like that. I bogeyed the ninth, after another wayward drive, and then I followed another bogey on the 10th with—how I hate to say this—a double bogey at the short (384 yards) par-four 11th. Once again my drive was right, even though I had used my three-wood instead of my driver.

So it goes in golf. I shot 77, which means I'm going to have to shoot about 67 to make the cut tomorrow. Afterward, I went to the range, where I hit some of the best three-woods of the year—pain free, too, with this new, abbreviated backswing I'm using because of the shoulder problem. Go figure. What was it I remember writing you a few weeks ago? If I could just take what I was doing on the range a hundred yards to the first tee. . . .

Anyway, if you'd been able to come this weekend you might have missed me—I have a sinking feeling I may be on my way back to Florida tomorrow night. I am realizing I need to follow my own advice here, which is to set goals I can meet. I remember giving a lesson to a friend whose game had gotten away from him, and he hit a few pitching wedges to a target about a hundred yards away.

"What are you trying to do?" I asked him as diplomatically as I could.

"Hit the ball," he answered.

"You already know how to do that," I said. "And if you didn't, I could teach you in half an hour. I could teach a monkey how to hit a ball in half an hour." And then I demonstrated, hitting the ball as hard as I could, swinging from overhead, as if to make the ball disappear into the ground. I sure did hit it.

My friend looked at me sheepishly.

"I know what you're feeling," I continued. "We all feel some version of that. Let's define a goal, one that makes sense, and then let's work on that."

That's what I need to do now—set such a goal. Golf is such a humbling game. Do me a favor and don't ever buy into those articles and videos that promise instant gratification in golf. There is no such thing, only moments of satisfaction inevitably followed by frustration, as if in a cycle. That's when you really have to bear down and count your lucky stars. I just counted mine and your friendship is one of them.

As ever,
Bob

19
The place

May 26

Dear John,

I'm sorry to bother you again, just after I wrote you from New Jersey. I'm back home for a few days; got in late last night after a hellish evening at Newark International (missed a late afternoon flight after getting caught in bad traffic).

Outside of sex, there is no greater physical feeling I know than hitting a five-iron flush. I've hit a few over the years, and if I never hit another one that matters I can step back and feel satisfaction from what I've been able to accomplish in the game. Of course, I'm working hard to find that feeling again, and I expect you to find it, too, at whatever level you take your golf. But there is something else I have been meaning to tell you, something I should have added in my letter from New Jersey, because it has to do with a totally different kind of feeling, more of a mental one, something that happens when you get inside the game so much that the "place" where you are playing golf, the space whose outer landscape we call a golf course, is actually an internal process. I was in that place when I won on the Senior Tour a couple of years ago, before the first of my injuries, and I've been there other times as well. I thought I was there in New Jersey, and then when I got lost I found my way again, except by then I was on the range, hitting those three-woods.

How clear my thinking was then. There is only a single thought, really—the shot at hand. You're by yourself, in your thoughts about the shot—you can see everything. One day I played Timuquana again, and on the sixth hole, a par five, my drive landed to the left, behind some trees. I had to hook a four-iron around those trees and then over some water to reach the green. I wasn't anxious. I wasn't analytical. I had my yardage (at Timuquana I know the yardages from memory), I'd checked where the pin was. In my mind, before I swung that four-iron the ball was already there, on the green, right where it landed a few seconds later.

Did you know that Ben Hogan, toward the end of his life, never played a round of golf anymore but he still went to his club, Shady Oaks, every day? There was a table in the dining room there at which only he could sit; if he didn't come in, the table remained empty. And then, after lunch, the great man would get some clubs, a bag of balls, and a cart, and head out to the far end of the driving range and hit balls. I met Mr. Hogan twice back in my days at Timuquana when I was on the Hogan staff and we carried his line of clubs in our shop; in fact, he autographed a photo for me and another for David. But I never watched him hit balls during my two trips to Ft. Worth. I am sure, however, from all I have heard and read and from all I have learned playing this game my entire life that I know where he was, what he was doing.

He was in that place.

Here's to you—
Bobby

20

Inner drive

June 21

Dear Colin,

You'd like it here, my friend. We're in Massachusetts, outside Boston to be exact, where we have a regular Senior Tour event starting tomorrow and then next week we move around the city to the north, to an old town called Peabody, where we play the U.S. Senior Open. I've never been there, but I understand the Salem Country Club course is another old classic, like Ridgewood, where we played the Senior PGA a couple of weeks ago. I'm hoping to get into the town of Salem, too, to see the witches' museum. Maybe those wicked old women can cast a good spell on my game.

What a mystery this sometimes seems to me, Colin. And yet—there are days when I am so certain I understand something, understand it maybe even better now than before—now because I have been playing hurt most of the past two seasons and I have had to discover the hard way how much this game is part of me—how much I miss it when I'm away from it, or about to be away from it, as I will be again after my shoulder surgery later this summer.

Today, I didn't even go over to the golf course to practice. Had breakfast at the hotel, where I ran into David Graham and Hubert and some of the other guys—there's a good field this week, with many players using the tournament as a tune-up for the Open. Then I went back to my room, fooled around on my computer for a while—beginning to get the hang of e-mail. In fact I told Shari we ought to get a new computer at home. And then I visited with a friend who'd come to watch me practice.

Maybe he was trying to cheer me up, I'm not sure, but, honestly, I don't think I was anything but my usual sweet self. Maybe he just wanted to talk. He'd been doing a lot of reading about golfers who've had breakthroughs, he told me. He'd come to think of a player's big breakthrough as the final one—you know, like me winning that tournament, that would be what he called my last breakthrough. I told him I didn't like that term particularly. "Makes it seem like it's all downhill after that!" I said.

"I'm happy to call it something else, then," he said.

"Okay," I replied. "I think it's called the place."

Well, he said he needed to think about that, but

could he ask me about David, who'd made—and he was about to say a breakthrough but caught himself—who found . . . "who found the place—your place."

"Of course," I answered. "What do you want to know?"

"How it happened."

"No one can explain that fully," I said, remembering my own astonishment and pride when he shot that 59. "It's part of the riddle of golf. But I can give you some clues."

Which I did, going back to the days at Plantation and then junior golf, when David started playing in tournaments. But first I explained to him what I saw as the difference between breakthrough and place, how one was related to the other but they were not the same. Breakthrough, to me, is a technical advance, a new achievement, a new capability or new competitive edge. But place—zone is the word you hear on TV—is more a state of mind, a concept of effortless flow. Place is the moment in which ability and challenge progress together, like two people dancing who always sense what the other is doing. Time collapses.

I remember we didn't have the money for David to travel to some of his tournaments—lots of the kids would fly and then stay in hotels—so I'd drive him over toward Tallahassee, south to Orlando and Miami, north into Georgia, where he ended up going to college. In college he didn't understand at first that even though golf is an individual game it's still a team sport in school.

I know he and Puggy Blackmon, his Georgia Tech coach, had some things to work out, especially during the period when Puggy didn't play David number one.

That hurt. So did playing in the BellSouth Classic, a Tour event, when he was a junior in college, and after the third round he was the leader. That wasn't the part that hurt—it was what came after. I'd driven up from Florida and was caddying for him, and before the last round he talked as if he thought he was ready, right then, to be playing on Tour. And maybe he was, in a sense; certainly he had the game, the shots. But his score that fourth and final round in Atlanta was 79, and it was back to school. He needed more time, needed it even the next year when he finally did leave Georgia Tech after being named the top collegiate golfer in the country, turned pro, and despite two wins that summer on the Nike Tour didn't make enough money to graduate to the PGA Tour. Another year in the minor leagues, with occasional PGA Tour appearances, finally got him his playing card (though he didn't win an event, he finished eighth on the 1994 Nike Tour, high enough to get it). In 1995, his first full year on the PGA Tour, David played in twenty-six events, made the cut in twenty, and earned almost $900,000—more money than his grandfather Hap probably earned in his entire lifetime, and about ten times what I was getting paid as a full-time club professional at Plantation. That, of course, was the last year I worked as a club pro. By 1996 I had started my new golf life.

Colin, you know some of this better than I do probably. All the second-place finishes David had at the beginning—three in his rookie season, two more in 1996 and again in 1997, and then—maybe breakthrough is the word, how he won the last three events of the 1997 season, four the following year, and four more in the first few months of 1999. And yet, with the disappointments that have also come, especially at the Masters, it would be too simplistic to use the word breakthrough. You build, it seems to me, in whatever you do.

You persevere.

And isn't that—how you put yourself in a position to make a breakthrough—almost like a parable of the virtue you have always extolled above all others, inner drive? Isn't that what you always said to me you noticed about David, back when he was a boy, after his brother had died and he started coming over to the golf course, day after day after day, and each day he would hit golf balls, hundreds and hundreds of golf balls—and he was just a boy? Where does that desire, that dedication, that ambition come from, Colin? I am his father, but I cannot answer that question. But I can see it, you could see it then and I saw it this spring, when he lost the Masters by the margin of that seven-iron at 16 and then—what is it about numbers in golf—a 7-footer at 18?

His day will come.

Cheers,
Bobby

21

Not the same without you

June 21

Dear Shari,

Just wrote a long letter to Colin and now it's late. Might walk over to the lounge for a nightcap, but I'll probably just go to bed. Not that I'm worried about missing my tee time—haven't set an alarm clock yet, not once, never.

It's not the same when you're not along. Golf for me was made for your company.

Love ya,
Bobby

22
Give everything

June 26

Dear Elf,

When you think about it, what have I done in my life? I missed serving in Viet Nam—wasn't even drafted. Like you, I became a golf pro and worked my butt off doing something—providing something for people who could afford it, giving them lessons and a good time. And I supported my family by doing it. You, too. But I didn't make anything, like a car or a computer or a loaf of bread, neither of us have. No product. And then I got lucky and was able to play on the Senior Tour. But like David says, what do we all produce? David just goes out and plays golf and then he gets paid millions of dollars. Why?

Remember those backyard rinks we used to skate on as kids in Schenectady? Those were the days when you had those shoes that always seemed to curl up at the toes, so we called you Elf. Elfie. When was it, probably soon after Christmas, I suppose, that it was cold enough, long enough that you could shovel off most of the snow in the yard, trample down what remained, then flood it with water from the garden hose. You had to work quickly when you brought the hose out, so it wouldn't freeze. Then the slush on the ground would harden, and more water would puddle up that would eventually harden and freeze, and after a few days if the weather held there'd be a rink. You were always a better skater than I was, and I never cared much for playing hockey when we skated. Probably because I wasn't that solid on my feet, though I did enjoy speed skating on the pond in Schenectady's Central Park. I had a pair of real speed skates, too, with those long blades. Man, I could move on those! Didn't have to worry about the quick stops and starts you needed in hockey, or somebody leveling you if you were looking the wrong way. Mostly for me, skating was a way to pass the time in the winter, before enough snow melted that I could begin hitting balls again. In March the rinks would be soft in the sun, and by late March or early April there was nothing left of the ice.

Gone, like a round of golf when it's over. And yet—if that were it, if what we did were like making that rink and then watching it melt, can you imagine devoting your life to it? I think it must have been Dad who first said to me, "The great thing about problems in golf, if you can learn to look at it that way, is this: It's all in front of you, nothing behind you. And the game is working that out, getting the ball from A, where you are, to B, where you're going." Sounds so easy, doesn't it, Jimmy? But as we both know, there are so many intermediary problems and other factors.

Wind.

Rain.

Bunkers.

Everything between you and your target. Eventually, if you work at it long enough, you get to a point where you're accomplished enough to have an idea of what you're doing. But that takes so long! Don't you find with your students this is the most difficult concept to communicate, especially with kids—how long the process takes?

One way of defining a good player—and this is at whatever level he or she plays—one way is how successfully they handle this concept, this idea of the time you have to put in before you're getting out of the game something approaching what you're capable of, physically.

But there's also the opposite problem, trying to do too much too soon. Did I ever tell you about that guy who was playing in one of our member-guest tournaments when I was still at Plantation? A good player, four or five handicap, and he introduced himself to me afterward and asked if I might give lessons to his son?

"I've taken him as far as he can," this man said. "I really want my son to move on to the next level."

"Well, yeah, okay," I replied. And then the man repeated what he'd said about getting his son to what he kept referring to as, "the next level."

"Oh, by the way," I asked. "How old is your son?

"Eight," was the stunning answer.

I told him to come back in a few years.

I'll never forget after I'd started working for Tommy Birdsong at Fernandina Beach, back at the beginning of my career, and someone came in wanting a golf lesson.

"What do I do?" I asked Tommy.

"You give him a golf lesson," said Tommy, a little incredulously.

So I got this guy started—he'd never played before—so I showed him how to grip it, how to stand, where to stand, all that stuff. Told him to keep his eye on the ball, keep his head behind the ball, keep his left arm straight on the backswing, all that wisdom of my twenty-one, twenty-two years. And I was trying to teach this guy how to do everything perfect. In one lesson! What an illusion that was. At the end of the lesson I was feeling terrible, because I realized I'd wasted someone else's time, trying to teach the impossible.

"Thanks," my eager pupil said. And he paid me my five dollars, which is what we got in those days for a half-hour lesson. "When can I come again?"

Can you imagine? What a lucky break for me, to get a student that nice, that forgiving. And right then I resolved to change my philosophy. Who cares how you look? If you accomplish your goal, you're successful.

And everyone looks different anyway, even on Tour guys have such individually different swings. Of course, there are things they all do—they all make that shoulder turn, they all get the club head squared at impact—but no one does it "perfectly." There is no perfect. No perfect golf, no perfect life.

A successful match in golf is not one in which you play great and win, I used to tell David. You might win the match even though you played badly. But you won because your opponent played worse. So, you're still called the winner. And in stroke play, I used to teach him, it's not how pretty all the individual numbers look on your scorecard. A double bogey might or might not cost you a tournament, because of what it adds up to with the rest of the holes. But the double—or triple—isn't what wins or loses the game for you by itself. It's just a number, that double, and if you can follow it with some birdies, it's what they all add up to at the end that determines how you did. Don't you agree, Jimmy?

I remember once I was playing in a tournament and my partner was John Schroeder, and he was in something like 48th place and I stood at 51st. We were out of it, in other words. And on the 16th hole I made a long putt for birdie, and I raised my fist, like it meant something.

"What'd that putt do for you?" asked John on the way to the next tee. "Moved you up a place, maybe. Made you fifty bucks, maybe."

"Well, fifty bucks is fifty bucks, John," I said. "And if

I make another birdie on this next hole, maybe that one will be worth a hundred. And isn't that the stakes we'd be playing for if this was a Tuesday and we were just out here practicing, with a side match to keep it interesting? So if fifty dollars matters on Tuesday, why can't it matter on Sunday?"

It reminded me of some of what I was taught long ago by the old guys who used to hang around Stanford when I was a kid. Man, some of them knew how to play. They might not have a textbook swing or be very long off the tee, but they could play golf. If the pin on a short par four was on the right and there was out-of-bounds along the right side, they knew to aim for the middle of the green on their approach, even if they were trapped in a tight spot along, say, the right rough. If they need two putts to win a hole, they never tried something crazy that left them such a long comebacker if they missed the first putt that they ended up three-putting.

A lot of what I learned about golf from those men they taught me with bets—matches where we bet. And since I was still in school, making not much money from Dad picking up range balls or, later, working on the grounds crew at Schenectady Muni, my access to funds was severely limited. We'd play a Nassau, maybe a quarter a hole, automatic presses if you were two down; but you could double press if you wanted to, and that was something these guys were masters at. If they were losing a match, they would wait for just the right moment to double press—say a long par three, with out of bounds on the left, where they knew there was a chance with my youthful energy I might overswing and hook the ball out. Somehow, on many matches when I was ahead, I ended up losing, often on the last hole of a match where there were so many presses out that I could hardly keep track of them.

I guess we both got our distance from Dad, who used to tell us when we were kids to hit the ball as hard as we could. That developed hand speed and, with the coordination of your body turn, we used to get it out there, didn't we? The rest—aim, action—came later, aided no doubt by all the darts we played. And remember how we used to pitch pennies and flip trading cards? It got so no one would flip against us, we were so deadly, especially with that deal where you had to flip your card against a wall, hit the wall, then land the card on the floor or ground with one side of it leaning against the wall for a winner. Remember in college when we went to the Tallahassee Fair and won all those kewpie dolls throwing darts at balloons? We had so many prizes they prohibited us from playing anymore.

Now that I think back on those days I understand better how Dad got his nickname. Hap—for Happy. It seems so corny when you try to explain that to someone, but we never looked at it that way, especially considering how strict he was. Think about him so much these days—how I wish, when he was still alive, we could have talked with one another about what I feel now, what I can finally see, the connection between all of us. Maybe, in his own grief over our family's loss, he knew.

So, in two days, on Thursday, I tee off again in the United States Senior Open. Just about all the great players of our generation are here. Today, I was going to play a practice round with McCord and his group but I bowed out, decided to save whatever shoulder strength I have for the real thing. Spent most of the morning on the range, bullshitting with the guys, trying to collect a bet someone owed me, listening to dumb jokes, hitting eight irons and wedges and some three-woods. Doug Sanders, who must be in his seventies, was hitting balls in the space next to me. He was wearing yellow pants and a sky-blue cashmere sweater, quite a statement. Reminded me of the guys on Tour when I was just getting out of college. Sanders kept asking me about the loft on one of his irons, something about whether or not it was correct. So I let him try one of my Titleists, and we talked about how the lofts on all clubs have changed over the years, making the seven-iron he hit in his prime more like an eight-iron today. But the more we talked the more I couldn't really figure out what the big deal was, all his questions, maybe he was just lonely.

Ate lunch with Raymond Floyd in the clubhouse, nothing special except the special atmosphere of an old-time club. We were north of Boston, lots of blue bloods. The locker room in this club (which must have a ten-year waiting list to get into) had been remodeled maybe twenty-five years ago. Guys can still smoke in the locker room. Floyd asked me at lunch how was I feeling after that pleurisy scare I had. Said I was fine, which I am, don't know why everyone made such a big deal about it. "You still smoking?" Floyd asked me. "Yeah," I shook my head. Why is it guys like Raymond Floyd think they have the right to ask you questions like that? Actually, he meant well. But hearing him speak to me like that made me think what a competitor he was. And Raymond Floyd was some kind of player in his prime. Those little chips he would make from just off the green. That funny move he had on his downswing. Deadly. Must have won many of his matches staring down his opponents. Can't you kind of hear him asking someone in match play, "You still making all those short putts for par?" And so of course the other guy misses the next one.

After lunch I grabbed a frozen yogurt bar and walked back outside with my putter; I'm still using the mid-length one, the butt-end sticks right up in your gut. Spent maybe an hour on the putting green, which is located on a small hill just above the downsloping, 18th green. I'll tell you, Jimmy, anyone has a putt from above the hole on Sunday to win the tournament, he's going to three-putt unless the USGA has relented and let the grass grow a little.

Even though Tuesday was a practice day there were thousands of people who had played hooky from work, driven through all the traffic, and were walking around in the heat and humidity at the Salem Country Club. A roar from the crowd signaled a good shot. I peered over the people gathered on the walkway below the putting green and saw Aoki, hands raised, standing triumphantly in the fairway. But a few minutes later the crowd groaned, and I knew without looking that meant Isao had missed his putt. I went back to my own putting and made a eight 6-footers in a row; the ninth lipped out.

It was getting hard to concentrate with the pain I was feeling in my shoulder.

I walked over to the fitness trailer, which was parked on the other side of the brick clubhouse in a small, cordoned-off lot beyond the second green. A huge throng was following the group of players just coming up the second fairway, and I could tell it had to be Jack and Arnie. Made me think of the fourth and final round of the U.S. Senior Open in 1997, held at Olympia Fields, Illinois, when I was paired with Jack. Starting the round we were both tied at five over, but then he shot 69 while I finished with a humbling 75. I came back a month later, though; tied for 21st in early August at the Bank of Boston, then finished tied for sixth in Long Island, and the next week I was second by myself at the First of America Classic in Michigan. Cashed a check for $88,000 that week, but what I remember now is the thrilling realization I could play with these guys. Two weeks later, in Pittsburgh, I was second again; this was the tournament in which Baiocchi beat me in a playoff. What a run I had then, continuing right into early fall. I belonged.

Now I belong on a trainer's table. That's where I've been writing this letter, waiting for the trainer, I mean. There's a line, if you can believe it. Chi-Chi's getting his back worked on. There were three or four other guys ahead of me when I got here. That's okay. I'm in no hurry. A friend came by for a visit, while I was practicing, and he stuck around for lunch, I snuck him into the locker room for lunch. Now he's gone. They'll be playing golf outside for a few more hours; most of the guys teed-off early, but there are still groups finishing the front nine. It's pretty neat when you stop and think about it, how we're here doing this, and all these people are here watching. I don't mean in an egotistical way, just the fact that something as inconsequential, if you looked at it from another perspective, can give this many people this much joy.

Someone stopped me today, on the way from the range, and said, "I'd give anything to be out here."

I nodded. I smiled.

"I know what you mean," I said. "I truly do." We shook hands, and I signed an autograph for him on his visor.

You have to give it everything, I thought to myself afterward. If you're really going to play golf—out here, at home, wherever you are—you can't give the game just part of your effort. You must bring to it your passion, your heartache, your dreams, your whole self. And you must accept what you receive in return. Somedays it will be a whiff on the first tee, or a buried lie in a bunker.

That same day you might make a 50-footer for eagle. Whatever happens, don't complain—and don't do the opposite either, don't start thinking when something great happens you've got it licked or, worse, that you deserved it. Just take it all in, the good and the bad, the feeling of being out-of-doors, the sky, the companionship, that incredible sense of being fortunate enough to play golf. We're all in the same boat, Elf, so let's enjoy the ride when we can.

Home soon,
Bobby

Bob Duval with Hap and Brent, age 11, in 1980.

I still run into people in every part of the country who either took a lesson from Hap or knew him, or their fathers knew him. That's how the line runs. It's like a good putt, straight and true.

Part THREE

A Letter to My Dad

23

You never know

Thanksgiving eve, 2001

Dear Hap,

Just back with Buddy. Parked up the road from the place David bought that he's fixing up; suppose I could have parked there, but somone was working on the house and didn't want to bother them. Anyway, Buddy knows the drill, going from the parking lot to the boardwalk. He does his business in the bushes, before we get to the beach, and then I let him take the slack from the leash and he runs at first, though that doesn't last too long if it's hot. He gets tired in the heat now. Getting older, like me.

You'd never guess what I was doing earlier this morning. Hanging curtain rods—which is actually something of a milestone in my recovery from the shoulder surgery

I had in August. I've started writing letters to tournament sponsors to get into tournaments next year. And a number of players have written letters on my behalf, which is very gratifying. Arnold wrote a note. And Gary.

Lately, with all this time on my hands, I've found myself thinking a lot about Brent. But last night I also had a dream about you. I was remembering things so clearly that when I woke up I thought you both were still here.

"Hey Dad, why don't you grow a beard?" Brent asked me in the hospital in Cleveland. So I grew a full beard for him. "The day you get out of the hospital is when I'm going to shave it," I told him. Remember how shocked you were when you saw me with it? I kept it on through his funeral. Didn't want to shave it off.

Brent was in a different school from David when he died. The boys started at Ortega Home Entry School, both of them. Later, David and Deirdre went on to Riverside Presbyterian and then on to Episcopal High School. It was a private school, almost like a college campus.

Brent was tall, taller and thinner than David, ran fast, and loved sports, especially fishing. Remember how he used to go down and catch mullet out of the river near our house? He loved the out-of-doors so much, especially bugs and snakes. He caught one that looked like a coral snake. Another time he caught a king snake and he knew it. He was never a Boy Scout, but all of us Duval boys were in an organization called the Indian Guides. Brent loved camping, and often we went camping with the other Indian Guides and their dads. Brent also loved to shoot. We'd shoot at the dump in back of Timuquana Country Club. We'd set up cans and shoot them with pistols and rifles that I bought. We also had special pellet guns. We'd usually shoot on Mondays, which was my day off, or we'd go out hunting for snakes. We'd always wear moccasins when we were hunting. Made us more authentic. David liked shooting, too, and after Brent died, he and I would shoot skeet sometimes.

Once, in Indian Guides, we built a totem pole in our backyard. We used an old telephone pole to make it. We painted it, working on it a long time. Then we had a campfire, sitting around it in a circle, eating hot dogs. Brent was kind of like Huck Finn, our friends used to say, or maybe it was Tom Sawyer. He had such a youthful interest in everything, even golf—which we played together, but not anywhere near as often as I would later play with his younger brother. When you played golf with Brent, he was liable to wander off looking for a tadpole in a pond, and we'd have to shout after him, "Come on, Brent, it's your turn to hit!"

Hap, I'm not doing a very good job with this. I don't generally talk a lot about what happened. I guess I'm a survivor, like you. You were always so resilient. You worked hard, saved all that money, and then you had a heart attack. Mom, your wife, had already died of cancer, and you never remarried. You took care of her when she was sick, and then after she died you moved down here to Florida with us. But that all came later.

I'd been at Timuquana several years by 1980 when my friend Doc Moore—you must remember him, Robert Moore, the proctologist—listened to me as I explained that Brent wasn't feeling good. Doc Moore was already a friend of mine, and he lived practically down the street from us. A very competitive person, a couple years older than me, he had just started taking golf lessons from me.

It was right after Christmas when we talked about Brent. Doc told us to take Brent in for a checkup, because he seemed to be tired, like he was losing his energy bit by bit. He was twelve years old, three years older than his brother.

So we got an appointment with Dr. Dave Johnson—he was a member at Timuquana, and one of the perks of my job was if you needed a doctor or a lawyer or anything else, all you had to do was make a phone call, tell them who you were, and you'd get right through. We took him to the doctor, who did a total exam, took blood and everything. We thought maybe he had mono or some kind of flu that just wouldn't go away.

This all happened in one day—from the time I talked with Doc until we had the exam with Dr. Johnson. What we'd been observing had been developing for a while, but when we called Dr. Johnson we took Brent to see him the very same day. And then that afternoon, after we got home, Doc Moore came over to the house, and he was there when Dr. Johnson called us with the results of his examination. Afterward, I found out that Dr. Johnson had called Doc Moore first.

"I've already contacted a pediatric hematologist, a specialist down in Orange Park," Dr. Johnson told us. We were stunned.

"I've made an appointment with him for you the following morning," Dr. Johnson continued. "I am not positive what it is that is bothering Brent, but I want the pediatric hematologist to take a look at it." I was no expert on hematology, but I knew just from the sound of it there was possibly something terribly wrong.

So we took Brent down to Orange Park, about 5 miles south of where we lived, and they performed a bone marrow test. That was very frightening to all of us. Brent screamed when they stuck a huge needle in his hip. We had to hold him down during the procedure. At that point, the doctors suspected Brent had leukemia. After the procedure with the needle, we waited and waited. Finally, the doctor came out and said that basically Brent's blood had shut down—the bone marrow that produces blood cells had shut down. They didn't know why. The name of the disease, which I had never even heard of before that day, was aplastic anemia. No one knew what caused the disease, and there was no certainty that it could be cured.

"You mean our son could die?" I finally said.

"Yes," was the answer. Then, silence.

It was one long nightmare for our family after that.

This was all during Christmas break, and Brent was still supposedly on vacation from school. He never went back.

Next we went to the Baptist Children's Hospital for more blood tests, and we were told they had to test everyone in the family, and they wanted to do it right away, to see who might possibly be a bone marrow donor. The only possible cure for aplastic anemia, we were told, was a bone marrow transplant.

This was all happening so fast. Deirdre was only four years old, but even she had to go with us, down to Baptist Hospital, to the hematologist.

I remember that after we had the blood taken, they gave it to me in an ice container and I had to drive to Gainesville to Shane's Hospital for testing. It's about an hour-and-a-half drive. So I drove down there and then came back. The test took a couple of days to be analyzed. I remember Brent was still playing with his friends—he seemed fine that day. Then the doctor called to say we definitely had to get a bone marrow transplant.

An oncologist we spoke with said there were three places in the country that performed pediatric bone-marrow transplants—one was in Los Angeles, one in Washington, D.C., and the third was in Cleveland, Ohio. We chose Cleveland, and they said they would put us on a waiting list for admission.

"You've got to be ready when we call or else we'll bypass you," they said

"How long?" we asked.

"It might be a week, it might be a month, we don't know."

I guess you block some things out, but I remember how badly David took it when it became clear that his bone marrow was the best match for the transplant. I was the one who told him that he was a match, and he started crying because he knew this was not going to be easy. And he was only nine years old. He understood that something was going to hurt—a lot. I guess they explained to him what was going to happen during this transplant and everything else.

We got a call from Cleveland from the doctor and they wanted Brent in two or three days. We wondered what were we going to do. How long were we going to stay? I had just bought a car, a Buick Skylark, and we drove to Cleveland because they wanted to do more tests on David. Grandmother Poole came down and stayed with Deirdre, who stayed home. It was a long drive, fifteen to eighteen hours, plus it was January and there was snow. We have snowy pictures of the trip on the way up. The doctors had warned us to keep Brent out of the cold because he had no defense mechanisms. He would never return to Florida.

So we drove up there. It was brutal. We stayed at the Ronald Macdonald House, one of the first ones built. Brent was at Rainbow Babies and Children's Hospital, part of Case Western, just down from the Cleveland Clinic on Euclid Avenue. There were more tests, which were extremely painful, with the same kind of long needle used on Brent. David stayed a couple of days and then Diane's parents flew up and took him back.

So Diane and I remained in Cleveland with Brent because the doctors had to do a procedure right away in which a stem-like device was pushed through his chest, all the way into his heart. And the doctors used radiation to kill Brent's bone marrow. Chemotherapy was initiated. All this time, Brent was a pretty good trooper. But he knew he was sick. He was only in sixth grade, still young enough to play in Little League.

I came back home a couple of times, but Timuquana's president said, "Look, Bobby, you do whatever it takes, and don't worry about things here." I really appreciated that. I had a good assistant pro who covered for me, and the club continued to pay me. I was gone for four months. They paid me, they raised $25,000 for our expenses, flying up and back. A golf tournament raised another $10,000. One of the members, Palmer Knight, was the trustee of it—we gave him all our receipts and he'd take care of it. That's what Timuquana did for me. It was just unbelievable—the cards, everything they did over the house—they took care of the kids. Doc Moore was with David a lot, helped him build a couple model cars while we were up there in Cleveland. I was building one, too, with Brent, just about when he started losing his hair. David had returned to school and played Little League baseball in the spring. His maternal grandparents, the Pooles, were watching him.

David had been on Brent's Little League baseball team. Brent had recruited him. Palmer Knight, who was administering the fund for our expenses, was also the coach of the baseball team. His son, Palmer, Jr., was a good friend of David's. Still is. They all grew up in Ortega. They're the ones that don't cut David any slack today.

I'm not sure of the time frame, but a couple of months passed. Brent was in the hospital all this time and we lived around the corner from his room. I slept in the hospital every night. Diane took the days and I took the nights. Then I slept during the days. The hospital encouraged the parents to stay. We helped with the nursing. By the time we left I could draw blood, I could do anything—I wasn't allowed to, but we learned how from the nurses.

Finally, radiation therapy was complete. We had to bring David back for the bone marrow transplant. Brent was lying on the hospital bed when they brought the bone marrow from his brother in a bag, just like blood, and inserted a tube into him, just like you would in any transfusion. Once the transplant was done the nurses stayed to monitor my son's vital functions.

After the transplant, David returned to Jacksonville. I think I might have taken him home, Hap, but I can no longer recall. I know I flew home a couple of times every month just to go to the club, to check in on people. Everything was going fine—the transplant, monitors, all the blood work. It looked like everything was going to work. So one day the doctors took most of the monitors off.

Our handsome, blue-eyed son was completely bald, so we got him a hat. The doctors thought he was recovering well enough to return home. But first, they said, we could take him out for the weekend, so we did just that. It was his last outing.

What brief happiness. We took him to a restaurant, but when he came back to the hospital he threw up the meal. We called the doctor and the next morning they did some more tests and said they didn't think the transplant was working afterall. Unbelievable. Just like that, everything changed for the worst, at the very moment when we all thought Brent was going to make it.

Back in the hospital, Brent's condition started going downhill very quickly. There was one emergency after another. I'd get a call to come over because he had another infection, a fever. They'd take blood and probe the bacteria to see what he was sensitive to, what kind of antibiotic worked and didn't work. Five or six times I had to sign for experimental drugs to be administered to him. Then one day he went into a coma, and they moved him to intensive care. Right up almost until that day, I think Brent was pretty optimistic. But then at the very end he was in great pain.

I was trying to get some sleep when a doctor called me. "It's time," he said. And I knew what he meant. I stood still with the phone in my shaking hand.

We knew Brent was going to die now. It was April, four months since he'd been diagnosed. The weather was just beginning to get warm in Cleveland. The ice in Lake Erie was melting. Opening Day for the Indians. Buds on the trees along Euclid Avenue, tulips and daffodils in the parks.

Imagine, all this effort to keep a twelve-year-old boy alive, and this fall several thousand people were killed in an instant when two giant buildings collapsed in New York after being struck by airplanes flown by terrorists. A lesson in scale, perhaps, but no consolation.

Grandfather Poole brought David up one last time to see his brother. David bolted out of the hospital.

"That's not my brother!" he shouted. That was the end of hospital visits for David. He flew back home. We stayed there until Brent died.

The doctors wanted to do an autopsy. We called the funeral home in Jacksonville and they arranged everything. The hospital was great about it, showing us every kindness. Then, the saddest day of my life, we packed up our car with everything we had accumulated in four months and flew back that night. Molly Murphy, one of the nurses we had become close to at the hospital, drove our car back to Florida. My brother-in-law, Bob Gideon, picked us up in Jacksonville and we drove home.

It was a big funeral, you'll remember, held in Fernandina on a spring day in the month of April 1981. There were probably a hundred members from Timuquana who drove over from Jacksonville. Brent's teammates from Little League were the pallbearers. Never in my life had I seen anything like it, nor would I hope to ever again.

Brent was buried there, in Fernandina. I've been to visit his grave a few times, but not often. I don't observe his birthdays. On his gravestone we had engraved a fishing pole.

Hap, I don't think I can write you about this anymore. "Play what's in front of you," you always taught us, and I taught that in turn to your grandson—your grandson the 2001 British Open champion. It worked out perfectly for him this summer at Royal Lytham. But of course it doesn't always come out that way. The past is always there. Brent still lives in each of us.

Now, when David and I are both home, we play as much golf together as we can. People ask me when I started David in the game. And I tell them I never started David playing golf, all I did was give him the opportunity. I just happened to be a golf pro, I say, so I had access to a golf course. How did I teach him to play? If by that you mean giving him lots of organized instruction, I didn't. He taught himself. He was observant. And I played golf with him, we'd be on the range hitting shots, and he'd see if he could hook this, slice it, do that. He'd try all those things.

Remember when we moved to the Plantation in 1987, there were four target greens on the range? One was 90 yards away , one was 140, another 160, and the fourth 200. So I'd say to David, "Let's see if we can take a five-iron—just that one club—and hit each one of the target greens." He learned that to make a 90-yard shot, you had to take the blade and open it up a little with the five-iron. We'd each do it. Then we'd try the 140-yard shot—still with the five-iron. It goes a lot higher, and sometimes it slices. The regular 160-yard shot was not long enough for his five-iron, but you could choke up and hit a really nice five. That was a good drill, it taught David touch and creativity. It taught him feel. The strength came later. Put them together and you have that six-iron he hit out of the rough on the 15th at Royal Lytham to win the Open Championship.

The times when both of us are in Ponte Vedra are rare. More often, I'll get a game with a couple of my best friends. We'll meet early in the morning, having breakfast at this little diner that I've been going to for years in Jacksonville Beach, and then head over to the Ponte Vedra Beach Club, the TPC, or Pablo Creek, where Colin's a member. You'd like playing Pablo, not just because it's a terrific Tom Fazio course, but because no one there makes a fuss about anyone.

We usually play a match we call a hammer. The rules are simple and brutal. At any time on each hole, if you've just hit a terrific shot or if one of your opponents has just hit a poor shot, you can say, "Hammer." As soon as you say that, whatever the stakes you've been playing for are immediately doubled. Now, the person you've just hammered can refuse to accept the hammer, but if he does, he automatically loses the hole. In other words, to stay in the hole you have to accept the hammer. There is no limit to the number of hammers that can be called on any hole. As you can imagine, very quickly, the stakes can get quite high for a so-called friendly match.

Going back to when Jimmy and I used to play at good old Stanford in Schenectady, I've always been able to hit the ball a long way, but these days David usually buries me. At Pablo, where we of course play from the back tees, there are several par fours of 450 yards or so. After a good drive, I'll usually be hitting a four- or five-iron on a hole like that, but with his tremendous length, David might only have an eight- or nine-iron. So you know who says hammer after we each hit our drive.

After I made the last shot and clinched my victory in the 1999 Emerald Coast Classic, and after I'd signed my scorecard, we watched NBC's telecast of the Players Championship conclusion in the clubhouse. David was leading. The night before, the two of us had talked on the telephone. David had reminded me of something that over the years I had taught him—something you had taught me—which is that you can't let yourself get too excited, or, too calm. Don't dwell. Don't project.

"I think you just learn to know what nerves feel like and accept them and kind of embrace them and move on," David said afterward.

He hit a pitching wedge on the 17th. Imagine, a pitching wedge and the pin was 140 yards away. The ball stopped 6 feet from the hole and your grandson made the birdie putt for a two that pretty much clinched his win. Dad, that tournament draws the strongest field in all of golf.

When I saw David sink that putt, making us the first father-son combination to win on the PGA Tour and Senior PGA Tour on the same day, I couldn't hold back the tears. My whole body started shaking. The celebration we'd already started would continue late into the night, and there were more parties afterward.

No matter what happens, you have to go on—with your golf, with your life. That's what you always taught us. Remember when Jimmy and I used to be shagging balls at Stanford for 25 cents a lesson? We were just kids, and we used to get tired by late in the afternoon. "Keep going," you'd say. "Don't quit."

That's something people need to hear today, after what has happened in our country and our world. But was it ever any different? When you were the only person in your family during the Depression who could get work—one person in a family of nine, including your parents. You got a WPA job. And you were happy. Grateful.

Dad, I feel badly for people who are afraid to be happy. It's okay to feel good about something, about having a drink with a friend, taking your wife out to dinner. Playing some golf. Because you never know what the next morning will bring.

Still going to physical therapy three times a week and

the gym now almost every day, but I've been hitting balls the last week or so and I'm going to play this afternoon. Colin's getting a group together at Pablo. The ball from whoever hits the best drive is the one I'll play for my second shot. Now that I'm getting out there, I wonder, will I still be able to do what I could before? How good am I going to get again? It's almost like I'm starting from scratch again. I'm a young golfer. But the shoulder's feeling pretty good, that's the important thing. I guess it's like anything else if you're lucky, the scar will remain but the wound has healed.

We miss you, you old sonovabitch.

With love from everyone,
Bob

Afterword by David Duval

The biggest thing in golf, the most important, is you can't be afraid of shooting low scores. It might sound silly to say—you know, obvious—but it's not. I think a lot of players at the professional level get to five or six under par in a round and suddenly they freeze. Instead of picking up two or three more birdies before they finish playing, they start thinking about holding on to where they are, to protecting that good score they've got going. But if you're going to win, you just can't be scared of making more birdies and going lower.

I know what it is to get lower—know it in my head and, more important, my gut. The reason I'm not afraid to go low is that I grew up around my dad and I saw it with him when we played, saw that he was never scared of shooting those low scores. And so, that's just how I got. Of course, it didn't just happen out of nowhere. It took some time like everything else.

Back when I was a kid, playing golf after school and during vacations at the club where my dad worked as the pro, I was generally let alone to discover things little by little. My dad never put pressure on me to succeed, in fact I don't recall that he ever once made me think I had to become a golfer, let alone a pro like him or my granddad Hap. The one special treatment I got was my own charge account for snacks, since at the club where my dad was the pro the members didn't pay cash for anything; they signed for it, and later got a bill. So I was allowed to sign for my snacks, which I must admit I thoroughly enjoyed; this was many years before I discovered on the Tour that if I was going to go low against my buddy Tiger and the rest I'd better get stronger and take care of my body like any athlete in a sport like gymnastics or swimming or track had to. So I started going to the gym; now my dad does, too. Like son, like father.

Anything to do with golf when I was growing up, my dad was always there for me. He took me to my tournaments when I started competing. He was there in 1989 when I won my first big event, the United States Junior Amateur. He was caddying for me in 1992 at Pebble Beach, when I qualified to play in the U.S. Open. I made him earn his pay that week. I didn't have a Tour bag like most of the other players, since I was still in school, so I used my United States bag from when I played for our country in the Walker Cup. That bag weighed just about as much as a regular Tour bag. I know my dad was working to carry it up some of those hills at Pebble, the long one at six and then the one at eleven, after the turn.

My dad's all right. We went through some periods when things were tough in our family, but we see each other a lot these days. I live part of the year in Sun Valley, Idaho, where I like to fish and snowboard, but I still have my home in Ponte Vedra, in Marsh Landing just down the street from my dad's new place. Actually, the quickest way to get there is by boat, along the Intercoastal. I know my dad loves his boat. Where I like fly-casting in a mountain stream or flying down that same mountain on my snowboard if it's in winter, he'll go out in that boat, sometimes with friends, but he goes out by himself, too, especially after he's been on the road for several weeks. You get like that, playing golf for a living, performing in front of all these people most of whom you don't know and will never meet; you need to be alone with your thoughts. Sometimes he'll come over to my place on his boat, but usually if he's on his own he might find a favorite fishing spot and throw his anchor down there, a cove somewhere in a marsh, or he might just shut the motor down and let the boat go with the current (which can be pretty strong where we live when the tide is coming in or going out).

I like to practice with my dad when I'm home. It's more interesting than just hitting balls, which I've never been one to do for hours and hours. With my dad, he can spot something in my swing pretty quick, and we can have fun making up games like we did when I was a kid, aiming for different targets, going toward the same target with different ball flights. It was my dad who let my swing develop the way it is today, with a little stronger grip than some guys would use, and with that movement of my head where it seems like I'm looking at the target again after I swing before the ball has left the ground. Someone else might have tried to change me, might have thought I needed a more "classic" swing, but my dad knew to leave me alone because I had something that worked—on the range and when it counted.

I think maybe in my dad's mind there isn't a whole lot of difference between those two places—in his mind. Naturally in his playing there often is; it's in the nature of the game, for all of us. But we strive to make it all one, and I think that's what my dad has been saying in these letters. The only "one," the only place to be, is right now, what you're going to do next. It's like what I learned from him about playing golf. You get on, he'd say; and then after that . . . you keep on.

In other words, whatever happens, you just have to accept it and continue, because there's no way you can go back and take the shot over again. And if it's a great shot, the same thing applies; you can't just repeat it; you might hit another great shot right afterward, but it's a whole new shot. That's a powerful concept. To me it means much more than putting the past behind you, which is a cliché anyway. And why would I want to forget where I've come from, what I've accomplished? You always build on what you've done, who you are. But the new day, the next tournament, the shot you have to hit right now must originate from something within you that knows—each swing, each moment—that this is the most important shot of your life. And then, no matter what happens, you approach the next shot the same way. Shot after shot, swing after swing, day after day. It's the same in your life, before you ever get to the green fairway. In fact it's how you prepare to play your best when you get there.

Think if you knew beforehand that you were about to die, that the next breath you took was going to be your last; imagine that was the breath you were going to take with you to eternity, whatever that is; as the seconds disappeared, as you sucked in your last gulp of oxygen, what air would you choose to breathe? So I think what my dad is saying, to take his theme, is that you can be a young golfer again every time you swing the club. But it's up to you; you can let yourself get down in the dumps, or you can fool yourself and coast—or you can make the greatest single decision of your golfing life, again and again and again. Yes, we're all going to make mistakes. But what you do next is truly in your hands. The one thing to remember, maybe the only thing, is *you have to choose.*